Metapolitics

Metapolitics

◆

ALAIN BADIOU

Translated and with an Introduction

by

Jason Barker

VERSO

London • New York

This book is supported by the French Ministry for Foreign Affairs
as part of the Burgess Programme, headed for the French Embassy
in London by the Institut Français du Royaume Uni

ïi institut français

This edition first published by Verso 2005
© Verso 2005
Translation © Jason Barker 2005
First published as *Abrégé de métapolitique*
© Éditions du Seuil 1998
All rights reserved

1 3 5 7 9 10 8 6 4 2

Verso
UK: 6 Meard Street, London W1F 0EG
USA: 180 Varick Street, New York, NY 10014–4606
www.versobooks.com

Verso is the imprint of New Left Books

ISBN 1–84467–035–X

British Library Cataloguing in Publication Data
A catalogue record for this book is available from the British Library

Library of Congress Cataloging-in-Publication Data
A catalog record for this book is available from the Library of Congress

Typeset in Monotype Baskerville by Andrea Stimpson
Printed in Mexico by Quebecor World

Contents

Translator's Introduction[1]

What is politics today? asks Alain Badiou, in this his most systematic treatment of the question so far. His immediate response – that politics is certainly not 'the political' – recalls the terminological distinction advanced by the jurist and political theorist Carl Schmitt. It was in the Germany of the early 1930s, in the context of weak parliamentary government and in the shadow of revolution, that Schmitt argued the case for a sovereign constitution in order to strengthen 'the all-embracing political unit, the state'.[2] For Schmitt, one might say that politics as subjective practice was quite simply irrelevant to the structure and endurance of political authority. In *Metapolitics*, by complete contrast, Badiou sets out from the premise that the State (generally capitalised here), instead of being all-embracing or totalitarian, is in fact something akin to a representative fiction, albeit a constitutive one.

It was in 1985, in his *Peut-on penser la politique?*, that Badiou would first highlight the fiction of State sovereignty, and expose the myth of the superiority of Western liberal democracy over the totalitarian regimes of the East. The intervening years, which have seen the people of the ex-Soviet bloc paying for this 'superiority' through hyperinflation, unemployment, corruption and widespread 'ethnic' unrest, have confirmed Badiou's point with devastating effect. For Badiou, the administrative collapse of the Eastern European nations could hardly be put down to the superiority of a capitalist over a communist State. Indeed, if anything, this collapse would merely confirm the historical precariousness of the State as a figure of democracy. For Badiou, the security of the political is imperilled – albeit unpredictably, and at odds with every 'democratic' norm – by the irrepressible resistance of politics.[3]

However, the situation is simultaneously more negative and more positive than it first appears. More negative because today those political sequences through which oppressed peoples fight for liberation no longer occupy a rightful place or enjoy any real visibility in our post-Cold War world. Instead, liberation politics is automatically read as a sign of impending humanitarian crisis. Despite this, and counter-intuitive as it may seem, Badiou refuses to be swayed by the contemporary 'crisis' of politics; a 'crisis' which according to Marxist common sense reached its 'high point' in May '68.[4] Why? Because on Badiou's terms crises are no longer either terminal or cyclical. In other words, Badiou refuses the very (pseudo-dialectical) notion of crisis. Today, 'crisis' affects the very condition of our social existence, and has become the stock in trade of 'legitimate' democratic representation, such that claiming high or low points in politics, while of interest to biographers and historians, sheds no light on politics *in actu*. To be more precise, 'crisis', from Badiou's standpoint, is nothing but the opaque sign of the absence or invisibility of real politics, not a systemic or epochal fact. The situation, however, is more 'positive' inasmuch as the putative crisis of politics, so far as Badiou is concerned, neither hinders its practices nor detracts from its core principles.

But what practices or principles can we expect from a politics that so often appears to provoke nothing but a mixture of cynicism and disbelief from the population at large? There is arguably a profound *lack* of politics today when measured against the revolutionary mass movements of old. But why should we take this perceived deficit as the sign of a hidden capacity for political resistance? This is obviously where a little more familiarity with Badiou's philosophy is called for.

Badiou's defining work of philosophy, *L'Être et l'événement*,[5] which informs the present collection of essays, arguably reinvents the question of being, and thus reinvents ontology. Badiou's theoretical starting point is nothing so empirically 'self-evident' as 'the social world'. Instead, Badiou begins with ontological axioms and procedures that subtract meaning from any putatively consistent world or situation, including 'the social world'. The name 'politics' occupies a special place in this ontological framework. Rather than 'being-in-the-world' – Badiou's ontology is *not* to be confused with Heidegger's sociology of being – politics is that which radically detracts, or subtracts *itself*, from all experience of what 'the social world' actually is. Badiou is not so pessimistic as to exclude from the realm of real possibility the type of radical political transformations that characterised modernity.[6] By presenting politics as a singular work, a mobile capacity that constantly defies classification, Badiou is able to hold on to such a possibility.

Nonetheless it must be said that Badiou's grasp is immensely strained, since his ontology operates in the realm of 'pure multiplicity', which is to say that it presupposes, as one of its founding ontological axioms, that 'Any experience at all is the infinite deployment of infinite differences.' Those unfamiliar with the various paradigms of multiplicity[7] should at least recognise the pertinence of the term for the articulation of complex, 'over-determined'[8] sets of circumstances. A world of infinite multiplicity could also be said to affirm the *un*determined nature of anything

and anybody; that, in Badiou's words, 'There are as many differences, say, between a Chinese peasant and a young Norwegian
professional as between myself and anybody at all, including
myself.'[9] In other words: if anything, nothing is certain.

But this 'nothing' – and this is the mainspring of Badiou's
ontology – is not to be taken as an outright negation. While
Badiou accepts, following Sartre, that the essential ontological
fabric of being is 'void', he still maintains that the 'ideo-logical'
structure of any given situation is consistent, and quite capable
of producing a reality effect. For example, although the proletariat of 1848 had 'nothing to lose but their chains', what
ultimately made them amount to *something*, or 'consist' in their
social being, was the internationalisation of their struggle for
freedom (74). Thus one responds to Leibniz's famous question
in the following way: there is something rather than nothing on
condition that the 'nothing' in question can be presented and
'counted as one'. Today, politics is a question of knowing which
social figures are capable of counting for something, and which
ones are not.[10]

For Badiou, then, the popular cynicism and disbelief with
which politics is typically greeted is no less of a political problem
today than it ever was. Moreover, nihilism, or the ultra-sceptical
attitude that nothing can be done, that no political alternatives
are thinkable beyond the 'laws' laid down by the global market,
is perhaps only a natural consequence of the extreme rarity of
'events'.[11] The French Revolution of 1792, the Paris Commune
of 1871, the Russian Revolution of 1917, function by way of
'political truth procedures' which aim to establish 'fidelity' to
events which have at least one thing in common, one 'common
denominator': namely, their resistance to any form of political
representation, even and especially if such resistance puts
their very political survival in question. An event can never be

guaranteed – although the suspicion that it never took place is hardly an obstacle to its veridicality. The fact that Badiou himself admits to being uncertain as to whether any event took place in 1968[12] by no means prevents us from *assuming* that it did, and on this basis drawing the relevant conclusions for political practice. After all, the threat of non-existence in a world of infinite nothingness, as Pascal came to realise, is to all intents and purposes futile.

But what conclusions does Badiou have in mind here? And what type of political practice is made possible from the point of such singular instances of politics?

I Politics Unbound

Badiou's first task is to distance himself from political philosophy, opting instead for so-called 'metapolitics'. While contemporary political philosophy is renowned for its claim to neutrality and critical reflection, metapolitics makes no attempt to seek ideological immunity for itself. We encounter such fraudulent behaviour in Kant's revolutionary idealism coupled with his distaste for the 'extremists' of the French Revolution (12). Today, the mere spectacle of democracy (and few are more skilled at waxing lyrical on the benefits of liberal democracy than the contemporary armchair philosophers) lives on in the work of Richard Rorty, whose preference for 'irony' over real politics is well documented.[13] For Badiou, philosophers are no more immune to political decision-making than anyone else, including those civil servants masquerading as politicians whose discredited grasp of public opinion is increasingly plain for all to see. Metapolitics is the apparatus for attacking this arch-complacency. Against political philosophy, metapolitics seeks to politicise, beyond the accepted limits of political theory, philosophical practice.

What then follows in *Metapolitics* is a series of tactical withdrawals from all forms of political representation. The inspiration here is clearly Lenin, although Badiou is at pains to qualify any such attachment. Not only has metapolitics no interest in the ways and means of parliamentary democracy, its militant thought-praxis cannot take the form of a party. The strange prospect of a 'politics without party' is accentuated in light of Badiou's hostility to communitarian alternatives (93–4), those self-sufficient minority support networks that fill in for the retreat of grand narratives from ordinary people's lives. On this basis, Badiou's present commitment to locally situated politics would seem to mark a subtle yet significant change in emphasis. His defining shift from global-systemic issues to local-situated ones has been marked, since 1985, by his active involvement in the Organisation Politique, a group of political activists committed to the struggles of immigrant workers living in France.[14] What political principle can a politics which supports illegal immigrant workers on the issue of residency papers, but which abandons any interest in the wider transformation of representative institutions (trade unions and universal suffrage), possibly fulfil?

Highlighting the 'dispersive flexibility' of Marx and Lenin's 'party', Badiou responds in Chapter 4 with the concept of 'political unbinding'. What political mass movements have irrevocably exposed, he suggests, through the lessons and experiences of 'May '68 and its aftermath', is the weakness of every form of social bond, whether it be party political or socioeconomic. Today the source of real politics no longer consists in recasting the bonds (by forming a more representative or democratically accountable party, or by amending the capitalist system *à la* Third Way reformers) but in their meticulous unbinding.

Despite the seemingly anarchist implications of renouncing the social bond with no specified 'ends' in mind – although of course one may remark that capitalism has never been more adept at exploiting its own 'revolutionary' potential than it is today[15] – Badiou's point here is that the political – as opposed to socioeconomic – 'breakdown' of community brings about the right conditions for collective intellectual work. No 'one' can determine what is objectively good for a community. The fiction of political representation, in pretending to advance the interests of others,[16] must therefore be swept aside in order to make way for the reality of political processes, for it is only then that a singular political sequence can begin to take shape. Political unbinding is therefore the creative act whereby subjects, in renouncing any outside interest (the so-called 'exteriority' of politics [40]), break with routine and begin to empower themselves as collectives.

We must give Badiou's radical conception of politics its proper due, particularly in light of its alleged abdication of political 'responsibility'. The charge laid by Daniel Bensaïd, for example, that Badiou's lingering fidelity to Maoism explains his refusal to acknowledge the changing nature of the contemporary political landscape,[17] presupposes exactly the kind of positivist dichotomy between project and reality that Badiou's philosophy renders meaningless from the start. The novelty of Badiou's 'thinking' politics lies precisely in its capacity to strip away the fictions of political representation to the point where any distinction between real and unreal, possible and impossible, collapses. Politics is not, as Badiou's critique of political philosophy sets out in the opening chapter, an overt lesson in pragmatism, or in how best to resolve social conflicts in order to reach a reasonable consensus. On the contrary, consensus is only ever the limited by-product of a singular politics, springing up in the here and now, held together through multiple and sometimes conflicting wills, and whose struggle, quite irrespective of the 'identity' of its subjects, has the potential to enter into almost any walk of life.

Unlike political pluralism and 'being-together' (18), politics has no substantiality or community beyond the real transformations it manages to bring about in any given situation. There are no historical constraints, no weight of tradition, no national, cultural, racial, ethnic, religious or corporate bonds that serve to limit the scope of a singular politics, for a singular politics has absolutely nothing to dissent from, react to or expect in relation to the situation at hand. In other words, it has no necessary *interest* in the situation. This is a crucial point which cannot be stressed too strongly. Not only are the subjects of a singular politics dispossessed in the above sense, they possess no set of demands which, once met, would bring an end to their revolt. Granted, what Badiou calls the 'political prescription' is aimed at transforming social 'contradictions' (e.g. racial discrimination, economic exploitation, governmental corruption). Indeed, prescriptions raise the prospect of real political change: that illegal immigrant workers in French hostels are entitled to unconditional legal status; that all UK students are entitled to a free education; that direct action by the landless workers of Brazil can win back land from the *grileiros*; that MOSOP can defeat Shell's commercial exploitation of the Niger Delta through a pan-ethnic alliance; that the ISM can prevent the Israeli army's demolition of Palestinian homes in Gaza and the West Bank; that the inquests of the ANWA(R) can help to eradicate the exploitation of women in Nepalese society through participation in Revolutionary People's War ...

However, it would be a mistake to regard these prescriptions as programmatic. Their singularity represents no one in particular and engages whoever happens to be in the situation at any given time. '[A]nyone who lives and works here, belongs here.'[18] For Badiou, the anyone in question means everyone in principle, not just those with the power and resources to implement a particular policy, those career diplomats whose job it is to promote the interests of their constituencies. On the contrary, politics is that which escapes those with the power to define what politics is. Henceforth politics evacuates ('voids') the arena of representation by subtracting itself, on a point of principle, from every representative fiction: that the majority of illegal immigrants are not 'genuine' asylum seekers; that fee-paying students are making an 'investment' in their future 'employability'; that the political activities of the landless workers of Brazil are 'criminal'; that the petroleum industry is bringing much needed 'inward investment' to Nigeria; that ISM members are naive conduits of 'terrorism'; that the question of women's liberation in Nepal is 'secondary' to the class struggle 'as a whole' …

For Badiou, politics reveals the discursive inconsistency of social statements and in so doing pierces through the common-sense fabric of the existing state of the situation. In this way politics *extends* the situation beyond the bounds of ordinary common sense. Beyond what seemed strictly impossible to begin with.

II Distancing the State

Politics is not out to take on the State directly, but rather to work around it, to 'put the State at a distance' (145) from both its local *and* universal conditions. The examples which Badiou has in mind here – the 'Soviets', the Maoist 'liberated zones', the 'gathering of the Organisation Politique and of the collective of illegal immigrant workers from the hostels' (152) – are meant to serve as 'models' for political reinvention. In this respect, those who believe that revolutionary politics is finished – because the government pays no heed to what people think – do not understand what politics is and what it is capable of today. The defining condition of the State is to exert power pure and simple, not only over those individuals who fall under its jurisdiction, but even and especially over those outsiders who do not. The State consists in the logic of a 'superpower' so infinitely superior to the situations whose parts it counts as one that any would-be adversary is always already foiled in advance (144).[19] As such, and so far as 'democracy' is concerned, the State observes the time-honoured tradition of making rhetorical statements: 'You, the people, have the right to air your views; and we, the ruling class, reserve the right to disregard them.' Unlike in the recent past, the State is no longer under any pressure to respond to genuine antagonisms in order to justify the consolidation of empires. It simply does whatever it wants under the benign pretext of providing security for human beings in a world of infinite uncertainty.[20]

The structural indifference of the State to all truth and the resulting implications for 'democracy' and 'freedom' are arguably the most pressing of contemporary political issues, although Badiou's treatment of them might be seen as somewhat cavalier. In Chapter 5 democracy is handled 'speculatively'. The question, Badiou informs us, is one of knowing whether and under what conditions democracy can count as a 'concept of philosophy', rather than as an object of urgent political rehabilitation; whereas, for its part, the question of 'freedom' doesn't attract any philosophical speculation at all.

Now, of course, this is entirely in keeping with Badiou's philosophical (or metapolitical) method. The idea that philosophy should stand in speculative opposition to politics, should *judge* politics, is precisely what metapolitics rules out. Metapolitics retains the direct action of politics in thought, and thus prevents the philosopher from interfering in a situation that can do without his exalted commentary. The point is not to interpret the world, but to change it. However, having said this, one wonders whether the shortfall Badiou wants to expose between a 'possible' world and the one we already inhabit is *more or less* likely to result in the advent of universal rights, as opposed to the dull repetition of particular 'wrongs'.[21] Jacques Rancière has good reason in this respect to suggest that equality, far from demonstrating the universal truth of the collective, is simply the disagreement waged between all and sundry for a bigger share of the social pie:

> Politics is the practice whereby the characteristic logic of equality takes the form of the processing of a wrong, in which politics becomes the argument of a basic wrong that ties in with some established dispute in the distribution of jobs, roles and places.[22]

Today, militant activists are by no means alone in attacking the spectacle of democracy, a fact confirmed by the clamour of countless pressure groups and parliamentary lobbyists, each seeking redress for a one-off instance of wrong. Confronted by this greedy spectacle, the militant might be forgiven for trading in his resistance to consumer rites for active participation in the least reactionary, most politically progressive form of democracy currently on offer. Is it perhaps conceivable that actually existing democracy, for all its 'democratic' limitations, holds out the possibility of a new and more dynamic set of responses to the capital–parliamentary settlement than we give it credit for?[23]

Nothing could be further from the truth. Badiou's outright hostility to such a 'concept' of democracy is axiomatic, and has in any case been stated more recently in no uncertain terms.[24] For Badiou democracy is intrinsically prone to the kind of liberal hysteria that wants to re-bind the Real to 'right-thinking' consensus. What type of 'democracy' is it, Badiou asks, that can bring the leader of the Front National, Jean-Marie Le Pen, to the brink of power at the French presidential elections of 2002? During such moments of seemingly monumental 'crisis' the people are quite capable of rallying the parliamentary politics of the lesser evil. But what type of parliamentary system is it that puts up with Le Pen and his ilk in the first place simply in order to cast its own racist policies in a more favourable, less 'extremist' light?[25] Episodes such as this confirm that fascism doesn't take root on the margins of society, but always emerges from within the existing status quo (in this instance originating from the acceptance of those racist politics generated by the immigration policies of Jospin's administration and those that preceded it – politics which, let's not forget, New Labour has outstripped in terms of both discrimination and brutality).

As for 'freedom', it is that which bypasses, as a matter of principle, this blinkered rallying to the 'constitution' in times of national crisis. The infinite 'limits' of freedom provide subjects with sufficient space to set about transforming their existing relation to the State during the course of a 'political truth procedure' (141–52).

As high as he raises the political stakes, then, for Badiou the choice remains no less clear cut: for politics to be thinkable it must resist, in more than simple abject resignation, the logic of the State and its accompanying 'democratic' hegemony, and in so doing raise the profile of political truths and justice.

III A Revolutionary Politics?

As a work of political thought-praxis *Metapolitics* stands out on its own. Who else in contemporary philosophy has the audacity even to attempt such an implausible reinvention of militant politics, let alone is capable of bringing it off? Like all true philosophical visionaries, what Badiou is able to detect with perfect acuity – and he is certainly the first to do this since Althusser[26] – is the way in which politics exerts its pressure in unpredictable moments whose consequences always lag behind events, and which today remain to be thought. Ours is the time of experimentation and reinvention in the process of thinking through these political thoughts. Badiou will perhaps forgive me, then, if I conclude with some very brief remarks which at the time of writing remain unanswered by his philosophy.[27]

Like Althusser before him, Badiou has certainly responded to the call for revolutionary theory as the condition for reinvigorating revolutionary practice. Unlike Althusser, Badiou has achieved this without being sidetracked by the thorny question of Marxism's 'scientific' status. As he states emphatically in his chapter on Althusser, '*Marxism doesn't exist*', which is to say that Marxism is no longer an objectifiable, homogeneous discourse. The truth-value of 'Marxism' is instead a *subjective* matter, one reliant upon the logical consistency of acts and statements which affirm the singularity of a Marxist – or 'classist' – mode of politics. Any such historical mode is prescriptive, thus opening directly onto the material determination of a 'place' in which politics is free to set its own limits. There is no need for any such practice to be named 'Marxist', and indeed to do so would be to sacrifice the singularity of political names (34).[28]

Badiou's 'nominal' Marxism is doubly at odds with more orthodox Marxist perspectives in combining a radical anti-

scholasticism (henceforth there is a founding separation between
political practice and any philosophy whatever, including a
Marxist one) with an immanent logic. Suspicions regarding the
'scientism' of this logic might be raised given the so-called
'numericality' of the political truth procedure (147). However,
any such suspicions would be misguided. For Badiou, science is
not 'applied' to anything, by anyone. As with politics, science is
in no need of philosophical mediation; the subject of a mode
of politics is no more in need of a supporting Theory or philosophy than the scientist who conducts experiments in his
laboratory. What we have in either case is a process of discovery immanent to the correct line of inquiry being followed, a
'line' (diagonal to the situation) which cannot be objectively
known in advance. In politics, 'only political militants think political novelty effectively' (62). For its part philosophy is the
apparatus for recording the truths generated by the political procedure – as well as Badiou's three other truth conditions of
philosophy: science, art and love.[29] The 'revolutionary' nature
of such philosophy might thus be gauged in terms of the seizure
in thought – through for example the classist mode of politics –
of the singular intellectuality of which a political subject is
capable. However, as Marx himself knew perfectly well (and it
hardly takes a genius to work it out), such seizures are not destined
to be the sole preserve of a Marxist philosophy, or even a class-
based political practice.[30]

And yet it seems fair to say that if a historical mode of politics
is to be genuinely transformative then it must involve a minimal
understanding – an 'apprehension' – of the existing relations
of capitalist production. For Badiou (knowledge of) capitalism
is unable to determine events, and so has no direct grasp on
political processes. Instead, capitalism is what prevents them
from taking place by converting the mutlifarious desires of the

masses into the 'objective' needs of 'individual' consumers.[31] Now, in maintaining as much, Badiou is arguably endorsing a reductive theory of individualism[32] that fails to take into account the potentially revolutionary affects of capitalist reproduction. As Marx discovered – and this is obviously where Althusser's own unique contribution to the question lies – the unbinding of humanity from the scourge of calculated interest presents us with the ultimate challenge, since such 'humanity' depends for its very being on the reproduction of 1) the productive forces and 2) the existing relations of production of a social formation.[33]

Consider, as a named component of this ever-pre-given structure, 'rent', which 'instead of *binding man to nature*, has merely bound the exploitation of the land to competition'.[34] In the context of a capitalist system that subsumes one and all and is under *no* condition subject to limits beyond which capital cannot reproduce itself, the prospect of founding a general – or 'just' – interest would seem to involve a fairly restricted conception of the true, *dynamic* nature of capitalist domination-exploitation.[35] To put the case bluntly, in failing to take the question of the reproduction of capital seriously, Badiou is prone to misgauge (for better or worse) the prospects for 'real' political resistance and social change. In *The Poverty of Philosophy* Marx alerts us to the danger when the only thinkable equality at stake, the only 'sovereign constitution' to speak of, is money: the unfixable 'constituting movement' of exchange value itself.

Badiou's characteristic response to the 'de-sacralisation' of capital is an ethical one. Writing in the spirit of Marx and Engels' *Manifesto*, capital is to be 'saluted', Badiou explains, for its 'destitution' of the social bond, its exposure of the 'pure multiple as ground of presentation'. Moreover, 'That this destitution operates through the most utter barbarity cannot disguise its

strictly *ontological* virtue.'[36] Certainly Marx's grudging admiration
for the irreverence of capital, for its denunciation of the One
and its profanation of bourgeois social relations, is indisputable.
But what is far more controversial is the suggestion that Marx's
'thought' of such relations entails no prior understanding of how
they are to be transformed (although, as Badiou would argue,
this lack of understanding by no means prevents such a transformation from occurring 'after the event'). Even if one accepts
that doing and thinking politics are unconditional, and therefore immune to such understanding, it seems to me that without
it the concept of revolution – i.e. that which interrupts the conditions for the reproduction of a mode of production[37] – is
unsustainable.

Now, of course, Badiou in no way claims to rely on the
Marxist concept of revolution – he even distances himself from
it[38] – and his decision to forgo it is no doubt made for some of
the reasons outlined above. Essentially, although admittedly I
am stating the problem rather simplistically here, 'revolution'
would only serve to frustrate a truly singular politics, bound up
as it is with the totalising practices of mass movements in the
wake of May '68 (44). Against the pathological desire for unity
and totality, for the definitive resolution of social struggles,
Badiou wants instead to tease out their 'contradictions' further
by pushing them to the point of *genuine* happenings. A singular
politics exists precisely in order to (re)think the concept of
'failure', and failed revolution, 'in interiority', i.e. in a non-
synthetic, non-dialectical manner (43–4, 46, 127). But how can
a popular struggle progress when, for Badiou, the political truth
procedure *and* the social transformation it claims to bring about
seemingly operate at the same level? It is one thing to say that
politics provides a place of ongoing resistance for subjects poised
on the *brink* of social change. It is quite another to claim that

politics is the site of transformation, actively transforming the situation into something *new*. But this is exactly what Badiou's metapolitics would have us believe. If 'revolution' and 'dialectic' really are the ~~remnants of old ways of thinking~~ politics then it is difficult to see what 'change' could mean in this instance. Arguably Badiou needs to set out criteria by which genuinely novel transformations might emerge through the course of political truth procedures without succumbing to statist config-urations.[39] Such criteria might then enable political militants to decide on the *type* of novelty at stake in politics today, rather than simply holding firm to truths irrespective of whether they offer new ways of thinking.

Marx's ultimate objective was the transformation of society – albeit by way of a 'transition' to communism that would no longer appear viable today. Whether such transformation was to happen 'all at once', i.e. as human perfection *sub specie aeternitatis*, or by degrees, i.e. on condition of the so-called 'revolutionary dicta-torship of the proletariat',[40] did not alter the basic principle that some sort of 'progress' should be involved. Such progress arguably lies at the heart of any would-be politics of emancipa-tion, since without the power to bring new worlds into being politics can only stand opposed, and has nothing to fight *for*.

Notes on the Translation

Badiou's thought distinguishes politics in the generic sense from any political orientation whatever. It is crucial to recognise that when Badiou uses the word 'politics' he is not talking about this or that variety: liberal politics, parliamentary politics, Nazi politics, Marxist politics, etc. For Badiou, the fundamental dis-tinction is between 'politics' [*la politique*] as singular thought, and 'the political' [*le politique*] as the politicking synonymous with capitalist-parliamentarianism. Likewise, 'a politics' [*une politique*] is a singular sequence – 'instances of politics' [*des politiques*] in the plural – through which politics as such is realised, rather than any particular variety.

Badiou's lengthy treatment of Sylvain Lazarus' work deserves a special mention. 'Intellectuality' [*intellectualité*], 'intellectual configuration' [*dispositif d'intellectualité*], 'that which is thought in thought' [*ce qui est pensé dans la pensée*] and 'thinkability' [*pensabilité*] all add up to a political discourse which is both rationalist and non-philosophical. Like Gramsci, Badiou sees political intelligence as that which shoots forth organically from within the situation, albeit without being directed by the party. *Pensé/pensée*: in those cases where undue confusion arose between the past participle and the noun I have opted for the verb 'to conceptualise' (not to be confused with the concept itself, which always sacrifices the singularity of a political thought process). The so-called 'places of the name' [*lieux du nom*], along with the places of science, ideology, overdetermination, etc., dealt with in Chapter 3, might strike those with little or no knowledge of Badiou's work as somewhat incongruous. But it is important to recognise that Badiou is speaking of places in the topological sense, not the geopolitical sense.

A place [*lieu*] is not 'grounds', or a ground, for action. Like a topological space, a political place is that which, despite undergoing 'continuous deformation', still retains the same properties. Like the homeomorphic spaces (sphere, cylinder, hyperboloid, annulus) that stretch into and out of one another while remaining geometrically identical, political places (subject, mode, name) are unaffected by superficial 'developments' in mainstream political culture, e.g. the formation of a 'new' political party. They are worlds unto themselves.

Elsewhere Badiou distinguishes between 'State' and 'state', the former denoting the political, the latter the ontological 'state of the situation'. The distinction is explored further in Chapter 10 where Badiou outlines the ontological characteristics of the political truth procedure. From 'State', Badiou derives 'statify' [*étatiser*] so as to cover both the consolidation of reactionary interests and general subjection to 'statist' rule. Similarly, 'statification' [*étatisation*] is one of the features of the Thermidorean betrayal that Badiou considers in the penultimate chapter.

Metapolitics is a book that develops some of the political questions arising from Badiou's major philosophical work *L'Être et l'événement*. As such it draws on many of the latter's key concepts: 'void', 'subject', 'being', 'event', 'situation', etc. *Événementiel* is now widely translated as 'evental'. 'Counting as one' [*compte pour un*] is the structuring principle of ontology which also re-presents or classifies the elements of a situation by subset or category, e.g. class, sex, race, party, etc. With *le réel* I have opted for the capitalised 'Real' in those instances where Badiou, following Lacan, is quite unambiguously referring to something other than mere 'reality', i.e. to that knowledge which lies always outside our grasp, but which we can come to know – albeit retroactively, after the event – by way of a truth procedure. Overall I have resisted deferring automatically to terminological conventions, aiming for a transparent political register unburdened, wherever possible, by the technicalities of ontology. After all, politics, as Badiou argues here, must ultimately be practised and thought in relation to itself alone.

My thanks to everyone who helped on the translation, most notably Alain Badiou, Ray Brassier, Martin Jenkins, Jean-Jacques Lecercle, John Theobald, Alberto Toscano and Stephen Waterman. Thanks to all at Verso for their support, especially Sebastian Budgen and Tim Clark.

Notes

1 My thanks to Alberto Toscano for his helpful comments and suggestions on this Introduction. Page numbers in brackets refer to the present text.

2 Carl Schmitt, *The Concept of the Political*, trans. George Schwab. Chicago: University of Chicago Press, 1996, p. 32.

3 Alain Badiou, *Peut-on penser la politique?*, Paris: Seuil, 1985, pp. 9–21.

4 See Martin Jay, *Marxism and Totality*, Cambridge: Polity Press, 1984, p. 360.

5 Alain Badiou, *L'Être et l'événement*, Paris: Seuil, 1988; *Being and Event*, trans. Oliver Feltham. London: Continuum, 2005.

6 Drawing on the work of Sylvain Lazarus, Badiou cites four such historical 'modes' of politics in the present edition: the French Revolutionary mode; the classist mode; the Bolshevik mode; the dialectical mode; see Chapter 2 below.

7 Badiou names two key philosophers of multiplicity who have served as counterparts and polemical reference points for his own project: Gilles Deleuze and Jean-François Lyotard. However, it is important to note that while Badiou dubs their approaches 'natural' and 'legal' respectively, his thought of multiplicity is mathematical in its approach; Badiou, *L'Être et l'événement*, p. 522.

8 The overdetermination, or excessive representation, of the complex social whole, wherein the economy is only determinant 'in the last instance', is Althusser's renowned contribution to the question of uneven development, and one of several acknowledged inspirations behind Badiou's theory of multiplicity. For a study of Badiou's possible philosophical indebtedness to Althusser, see Jason Barker, *Alain Badiou: A Critical Introduction*, London: Pluto Press, 2002, esp. Chapters 1 and 3.

9 Alain Badiou, *Ethics. An Essay on the Understanding of Evil*, trans. Peter Hallward. London: Verso, 2001, pp. 25, 26.

10 The *subjective* figure that Badiou has in mind is the 'figure of the worker'; see pp. 40–2 below.

11 See Alain Badiou, *Manifeste pour la philosophie*, Paris: Seuil, 1989, pp. 33–40.

12 See Alain Badiou, 'Being by Numbers', interview with Lauren Sedofsky in *Artforum* 33.2, October 1994, p. 123.

13 See Richard Rorty, *Contingency, Irony and Solidarity*, Cambridge: Cambridge University Press, 1989.

14 A regular update on the campaigns and slogans of the Organisation Politique can be found at: http://organisationpolitique.com where the Organisation's quarterly bulletin *La Distance Politique* can also be downloaded.

15 Such 'revolutionary' potential casts doubt on whether capitalism *as such* can be the counterpart of a figure of genuine political antagonism. As Alberto Toscano notes, there is a significant distinction yet to be made between the presumed aims of anti-capitalism (rejection of the logic of surplus value) and politics in Badiou's sense (distance from statist configurations). Indeed, the ubiquity of commercial rationale leads us to question whether capitalism can really count as a unified system of social representation at all, beyond its unstable channelling of particular corporate interests. See Alberto Toscano, 'From the State to the World? Badiou and Anti-Capitalism', in *Communication and Cognition* 37.3/4, 2004, pp. 199–233.

16 Badiou is hostile to the concept of 'otherness' and explicitly rejects the cultural studies-inspired approach to social harmony through 'tolerance' and 'respect for differences'. See Badiou, *Ethics*.

17 Daniel Bensaïd, 'Alain Badiou and the Miracle of the Event', in *Think Again. Alain Badiou and the Future of Philosophy*, ed. Peter Hallward. London: Continuum, 2004, pp. 94–105.

18 Alain Badiou, 'What Is to Be Thought? What Is to Be Done?', in *Whorecull* 3, November 2002, p. 15. The statement relates to the

campaigns of the Organisation Politique in their support for asylum seekers living in French hostels, but could easily be extended to any situation in which *figures ouvrières* are found to be under threat.

19 If the State is today a security provider, a 'Repressive' or 'Ideological State Apparatus', rather than a political adversary, then one might ask why political militants need retain a concept of the State at all in order to do politics. See Jason Barker, 'De l'État au maître: Badiou et le post-marxisme', in *Alain Badiou: de l'ontologie à la politique*, eds B. Besana and O. Feltham. Paris: l'Harmattan, 2005.

20 For example, the current US National Security Strategy sets out 'nonnegotiable demands of human dignity' under constitutional conditions as inalienable as the demands themselves. Gone is all mention of the 'Consent of the Governed' as it appeared in the US Declaration of Independence, 'the Right of the People to alter or abolish [the Government]' when it abuses its powers over them and usurps their rights. See: http://www.whitehouse.gov/nsc/ nss.html.

21 See Jacques Rancière, *Disagreement. Politics and Philosophy*, trans. Julie Rose. Minneapolis: University of Minnesota Press, 1999. Badiou discusses the book in Chapter 8 below.

22 Ibid., p. 35; translation modified.

23 Here one could cite Stuart Hall's attempt to rethink Marxism for the Thatcher era through his New Left reading of Gramsci. Such a move would qualify Hall, on Badiou's criteria, as a 'Thermidorean', i.e. a renegade. Cf. Stuart Hall, 'Gramsci and Us', in *The Hard Road to Renewal: Thatcherism and the Crisis of the Left*, London: Verso, 1988; and Chapter 9 below.

24 '[T]he enemy today is not called Empire or Capital. It is called Democracy. With this term we mean not only the empty form of the "representative system", but even more the modern figure of equality, reduced to equality before the offer of the market, rendering every individual equal to any other on the sole basis of virtually being, like anyone else, a consumer.' Alain Badiou,

'Prefazione all'edizione italiana', *Metapolitica*, trans. M. Bruzzese. Naples: Cronopio, 2002, pp. 9–15. Thanks to Alberto Toscano for his translation of this extract from the Italian.

25 Badiou, 'What Is to Be Thought? What Is to Be Done?'.

26 Badiou's canonical politico-philosophical reference point is Althusser's *Lenin and Philosophy and Other Essays*, trans. Ben Brewster. London: NLB, 1971. See also Chapter 3 below.

27 It is anticipated that Badiou will address some of the following issues on capitalism in his forthcoming *Logiques des mondes*, a sequel to his *L'Être et l'événement*.

28 See also Jason Barker, 'The Topology of Revolution', in *Communication and Cognition* 36.1/2, 2003, pp. 61–72.

29 See Alain Badiou, *Conditions*, Paris: Seuil, 1992.

30 Whether the classist mode of politics is, generally speaking, still salvageable today is highly debatable, although Badiou himself has long been of the view that 'of course it is essential to renounce the system of dialectical materialism, which has cemented the "classist" vision of politics'. See Alain Badiou, 'L'être, l'événement, la militance', interview with Nicole-Édith Thévenin, *Futur antérieur* 8, 1991. Available at: http://multitudes.samizdat.net/ article.php3?id_article= 620.

31 See Badiou, *Ethics*, pp. 105–6.

32 One is inclined to equate it with the naive anthropology of man which, in Hegel's philosophy, separates political society from civil society or the 'sphere of needs'. See Louis Althusser and Étienne Balibar, *Reading Capital*, trans. Ben Brewster. London: NLB, 1970, pp. 162–3.

33 Louis Althusser, *Sur la reproduction*, Paris: Presses Universitaires de France, 1995, p. 74.

34 Karl Marx, *Misère de philosophie. Réponse à la Philosophie de misère de M. Proudhon*. Préface par Friedrich Engels. Paris: V. Giard & E. Brière, 1896, p. 222.

35 Antonio Negri and Michael Hardt elaborate this idea at some length in *Empire*, Cambridge, Mass.: Harvard, 2000; and in *Multitude*, New York: Penguin, 2004.

36 Alain Badiou, *Manifeste pour la philosophie*, Paris: Seuil, 1989, p. 37.

37 See Althusser, *Sur la reproduction*, pp. 182–3.

38 'A lot of young activists [in the 1960s] spontaneously tried to name what was happening through the Marxist vocabulary of class, or to inscribe it in the logic of a new party, or used the signifier "revolution," etc. But these words were inadequate for what was happening.' Badiou, 'Being by Numbers'.

39 Sam Gillespie makes the same point in relation to Badiou's ontology in 'Beyond Being: Badiou's Doctrine of Truth', in *Communication and Cognition* 36.1/2, 2003, pp. 5–30.

40 As McLellan observes, the term seldom appears in Marx's published work, but when it does the emphasis is on a limited time frame. David McLellan, *The Thought of Karl Marx*, 2nd edn. London: Macmillan, 1980, pp. 229–30.

Preface to the English Edition

I

Since *Manifesto for Philosophy*[1] I have maintained that there are four philosophical conditions: science, love, art and politics. Equally I defend the idea that these four conditions are truth procedures. In their particular way they *produce* truths. Thus, philosophy operates on the basis of multiple truths, and certainly does not generate them itself.

There are three important consequences of this conception:

1. Philosophy, which requires the deployment of four conditions, cannot specialise in any one of them. I am opposed to every academic division of philosophy into would-be objective domains: there is nothing legitimate, or interesting, in what is termed 'epistemology' (philosophy of sciences), 'aesthetics' (philosophy of art), 'psychology' (philosophy of affects) or 'political philosophy' (philosophy of the practices of power).

2. However, philosophy maintains strict and singular relations with these conditions. It is twisted by these truth conditions: it points to their creative novelty in accordance with a concept of Truth (recreated by every significant philosophy)

that it initially extracts from the truth procedures themselves. In this way the truths are both the source and the target of philosophy.

3. Philosophy can only evaluate the general concept of Truth that it invents by submitting this concept to the trial of its own contemporary truth procedures. Philosophical evaluation requires one to circulate between the concepts it creates and its contemporary development of real truths [*vérités réelles*]. Thus, philosophy readily devotes itself to the arts, to the sciences, to love, to instances of politics, not in order to think their objective nature, or to standardise their practice, but in order to constitute itself as an experimentation of a new concept of truth.

This is the reason why I have multiplied the inquests into truth procedures: in the arts (theatre, dance, cinema, poems …), in the paradoxes of love (in constant discussion with psychoanalysis), in the sciences (especially 'fundamental' mathematics) and in politics. If one finds an emphasis in my writings – in restricting myself to the deceased – on proper names such as Cantor, Mao Tse-tung, Mallarmé, Lacan, Beckett, Murnau, Marx, Saint Paul, Celan or Robespierre, it is only because justice is done to philosophy only if philosophy itself does justice to its conditions and accepts being exposed to their inventive violence.

It was in this spirit that I published, between 1992 and 1998, a series of articles and books drawn up in accordance with the aforementioned truth procedures:

- I devoted two complementary texts to love, one reserved for *Conditions* ('What is Love?'[2]), whilst the other ('La Scène du Deux') was published in the collection which appeared as *De l'amour*.[3]

- In *Court traité d'ontologie transitoire*[4] I considered the relation between the branches of mathematics that presume to be able to provide a foundation for all of mathematics: post-Cantorian set theory and category theory since Eilenberg and Mac Lane.
- In *Handbook of Inaesthetics*[5] I proposed a sequence of conceptual incorporations of diverse artistic creations.
- Finally, *Metapolitics*, which is the present book.

In all of these cases the truth procedures are convoked, first as conditions for the elaboration of new philosophical concepts ('pure multiple', 'trans-being', 'appearance', 'state of the situation', 'numericality of a procedure', etc.), and also as a retroactive evaluation of the pertinence of these concepts when it comes to designating both the singularity of the True and its alliance with the times.

The words 'inaesthetic', 'transitional ontology', 'metapolitics' are coined against 'aesthetics', 'epistemology' and 'political philosophy' respectively in order to indicate the twisted relation of the condition/evaluation pairing, and, if possible, in order to deny oneself the temptation to rely on the reflection/object relation.

How does this relate more particularly to metapolitics?

II

Metapolitics harbours a political trajectory which may be unfamiliar to an English, American or Australian reader, although Jason Barker, in the book he devoted to my work,[6] provides its best account. I shall summarise this trajectory in four periods:

- Prior to 1965, there were two main political problems for a French intellectual. First, what position should one adopt towards the very powerful French Communist Party (the PCF), which controlled the most active workers' union (the CGT)? Second, what was the most effective means of engagement against terrible colonial wars, especially the Algerian War (1954–62)?

- What we might call the 'red decade' lasted from 1966 to 1976; it stemmed from the intellectual effect of the Sino–Soviet ideological conflict and the Cultural Revolution, and was followed decisively by the events of May 1968 and their aftermath. Its watchwords were those of Maoism: direct joining of forces by intellectuals and mass workers; 'it is correct to revolt'; 'down with the bourgeois university'; 'down with the PCF revisionists'; creations of autonomous organisations in the factories against the official unions; defensive revolutionary violence in the streets against the police; elections, betrayal!; and so on. Everyday life was entirely politicised; daily activism was the done thing.

- From 1976 to 1995 (and often beyond that) a lengthy counter-revolutionary political and intellectual sequence occurred, from the 'new philosophy' to electoral debates, under the direction of former Maoists. This was the bitter period of betrayal, which went by way of undifferentiated praise for 'human rights', the devastating critique of 'totalitarianism', the rallying to bourgeois parliamentarianism, the support for apparently humanitarian (but in reality imperialist) 'interventions', and finally capitulation the world over to American arrogance. This completes a cycle when one recalls that at the end of the 1960s Maoist militarism was originally deployed in support of the Vietnamese people in their ferocious war against the Americans and their puppets.

One of the singularities that I shared with my friends from the UCFML (1970–85), and with those from the Organisation Politique (1985–present), is to have yielded nothing to the current of counter-revolutionary betrayal. Certainly, we have modified the intellectual framework of our political commitment from top to bottom. But we have done so by accepting the revolutionary past, and at a time when opinion is almost unanimous in considering it a deadly illusion.

• From 1995 (which saw the great strike and protest movement of December) to today, a slow and tortuous evolution has taken shape, which intersects dramatic reactionary phenomena (racism, hostility towards the Arab world, violent defence of Western consumer comforts, unchained Zionism …) with a progressive recovery, perceptible among youth (a renewed interest in the experiences of the 1960s, massive hostility towards American hegemony …). Of course, this progressivism is sacrificed by the disastrous alliance of economic reformism and the vain adventurism of 'movements', an alliance whose strange name is 'Other-worldism' [*altermondialisme*]. I hope this book will help to make sense of the impasse towards which the inhabitants of the immanent 'multitudes' of 'Empire' lead their followers. That being said, the fact that political recoveries are always weak and confused to begin with is a law of history. What counts is the future juncture – although for the illegal immigrant workers [*ouvriers sans papiers*] this is already a reality – between a new political thought and organised popular detachments. After twenty years of sombre reaction and fierce counter-currents, when merely standing firm was a difficult enough virtue, we find ourselves amid the vicissitudes of reconstruction.

III

The metapolitical essays that you are about to read are of four types:

1. Polemical essays. These are directed against the academic, parliamentary and 'anti-totalitarian' right, which works in support of our so-called 'democracies' in the parochial name of 'political philosophy'. This is the most straightforward of polemics: 'Down with political philosophy!'

They are also directed against thoughts much closer in their proximity to mine, thoughts of friends and companions, but from whom it was a matter of firmly parting company in order to clarify the paths of contemporary political radicalism. This is the case with the articles devoted to Althusser (regarding the philosophy/politics relation between 1965 and 1975) and Jacques Rancière (which concern the possibility of an egalitarian politics between 1975 and 1995).

2. Essays of commentary and support. What is at stake here are the direct connections that metapolitics uncovers within political intellectuality itself. The typical example is the long essay devoted to the work of Sylvain Lazarus.

3. The examinations of major categories of political thought. Here, three in particular are re-examined with a certain meticulousness: 'masses', 'party' and 'democracy'.

4. Philosophical propositions concerning the modes of inscription of the political condition in the general system of truth procedures. This is the most important essay in the book: the last.

One has thus a series of variations, among which the reader can choose according to her own particular commitments and questions, even if these variations are presented within a framework which proceeds, in sum, from polemical exercises and elementary clarifications to the riskiest speculative hypotheses.

IV

The political history of English-speaking countries is by no means familiar with Maoist extremism of the 1960s (apart from in the militarised, rather than political, form of the Black Panthers and the Weathermen), or with the reactionary violence of the 1980s. Certainly, their governments could be particularly aggressive in the service of 'capitalist modernity': Thatcher breaking the miners' strike; Reagan dismantling the Welfare State; the two Bushes sending their gangs of military rough-necks everywhere; Blair's 'Thatcherism with a human face' … But their critical intellectuals, who although not having gone to the lengths of taking up positions as factory workers in the 1960s, did not become advocates en masse of capitalist-parliamentarianism during the 1980s or racist enemies of the Arab world either. The demonstrations in London against the war in Iraq bore witness to a confidence far greater than in Paris; and in the USA the text 'Not in our name' attested to an intellectual consistency less mediocre. This is what one might call the French paradox: intellectuals there are capable of great radicalism, but they are also fickle and highly dependent on prevailing phenomena. Quick to take to the stage, they rarely enjoy the lengthy and obscure tenacity of political constructions.

The present book joins forces against this shameful fickleness. It shows the extent of my convictions, and not simply their intensity. I am happy that it is appearing in English, for I have found there to be, in the countries which speak this language, perhaps less certitude and audacity, but more tenacity.

Los Angeles, 14 December 2003

Notes

1 Alain Badiou, *Manifesto for Philosophy*, trans. Norman Madarasz. Albany: SUNY, 1999.

2 Alain Badiou, 'Qu'est-ce que l'amour?', in *Conditions*, Paris: Seuil, 1992; translated as 'What is Love?' by Justin Clemens, in *Umbr(a): A Journal of the Unconscious*, 1, 1996; reprinted in R. Salecl ed., *Sexuation*, Durham, NC: Duke University Press, 2000.

3 Alain Badiou, 'La Scène du Deux', in Badiou et al., *De l'amour*, Paris: Flammarion, 1999.

4 Alain Badiou, *Court traité d'ontologie transitoire*, Paris: Seuil, 1998.

5 Alain Badiou, *Handbook of Inaesthetics*, trans. Alberto Toscano. Stanford: Stanford University Press, 2004.

6 Jason Barker, *Alain Badiou: A Critical Introduction*, London: Pluto Press, 2002.

By 'metapolitics' I mean whatever consequences a philosophy is capable of drawing, both in and for itself, from real instances of politics as thought. Metapolitics is opposed to political philosophy, which claims that since no such politics exists, it falls to philosophers to think 'the' political.

A.B., April 1998

Prologue

Resistant Philosophers

I would like to name, at the beginning of this book about how philosophy grasps politics, the first person to teach me how philosophy grasps science – Georges Canguilhem, who died a few years ago now and who, as a consummate example of a philosopher of Resistance, deserves our unqualified homage.

Canguilhem was not the type of man to make a lot of fuss about his feats of arms, which were nevertheless as real as they were consistent. In this respect he was like many Resistance figures, whose personal and political silence on their action was the measure of this simultaneously radical and intimate, violent and reserved, necessary and exceptional action. It was not resistant subjectivity, we know, which took pride of place in the 1950s. The silence of a good number of Resistance figures was one aspect of a widely shared political conviction which felt under no obligation to clarify its involvement, either in the collapse of the Third Republic, or in the allegiance to Pétain, or on the question, which today is making a comeback, of the continuity of the State administration even in abject circumstances.

President Mitterrand, in whose honour we had to endure the decree of a national day of mourning, came to defend positions regarding precisely these points – the State, Pétainism and the Resistance – in terms which contrast sharply, in both form and content, in their presidential solemnity and public appeal, with the prolonged silence of Canguilhem and many others.

The fact is that the object of our national mourning belonged to that widespread species of political tacticians for whom it was natural to be a Pétainist 'along with everyone else', and then to become a Resistance figure as circumstances changed, and then go on to become a good many other things besides, so long as they went with the times or allowed themselves sufficient room for manoeuvre.

The declaration of a national day of mourning suggests that there are good grounds for commemorating something that, although national, is no less worthy of universal public celebration.

Let's just say, so as to respect as we always must the peaceful repose of the dead, that I prefer to celebrate, under the sign of the national (I love my country, or rather: I love what it is sometimes capable of), Georges Canguilhem, Jean Cavaillès or Albert Lautman rather than François Mitterrand.

If he was silent about himself then Georges Canguilhem was certainly not silent about other people, other philosophers involved in the Resistance. Occasionally we should reread the little volume that originally appeared in 1976, as a limited edition of 464 numbered copies, under the title *Vie et mort de Jean Cavaillès*.[1]

There we find the speeches Canguilhem made to mark the opening of the Jean-Cavaillès Amphitheatre in Strasbourg in 1967, of a commemoration at the ORTF[2] in 1969, and one at the Sorbonne in 1974. Canguilhem sums up the life of Jean Cavaillès: philosopher and mathematician, professor of logic, cofounder of the Resistance movement Libération-Sud, founder of the Cahors military action network, arrested in 1942, escaped, arrested anew in 1943, tortured and shot. He was identified only as 'Unknown no. 5' when discovered in a mass grave, in a corner of the citadel of Arras.

But what Canguilhem wants to re-establish goes much deeper than the obviously heroic qualities of his subject ('A philosopher-mathematician stuffed with explosives, a man as lucid as he was courageous, a man both resolute and without optimism. If that isn't a hero, what is?'[3]). Faithful, in fact, to his own methodology – the identification of patterns of coherence – Canguilhem seeks to clarify the connections between the philosophy of Cavaillès, his political commitment and his death.

It is true that this is an apparent enigma, since Cavaillès was working quite some way away from political theory or committed existentialism, in the field of pure mathematics. And even more so since he thought that the philosophy of mathematics had to rid itself of all reference to a constituent mathematician-subject, in order to examine the internal necessity of notions. The now famous final sentence of the essay *Sur la logique et la théorie de la science*[4] (a text drafted during his first imprisonment in the camp of Saint-Paul-d'Eygaux, where the Pétainist State had placed him) states that the philosophy of consciousness should be substituted by the dialectic of concepts. Here Cavaillès anticipated by twenty years the philosophical endeavours of the 1960s.

Moreover, it was precisely in this demand for rigour, in this intellectual cult of necessity, that Canguilhem saw the unity of Cavaillès' commitment and of his logician's practice. It was because, following Spinoza, Cavaillès wanted to de-subjectify knowledge that in the same spirit he considered resistance to be an inescapable necessity that no reference to the self could circumvent. Thus he declared in 1943: '"I am a Spinozist, I believe that we are seized by necessity everywhere. The logical processes of mathematicians are necessary, even the stages of mathematical science are necessary, and likewise this struggle that we are leading.'"[5]

And so Cavaillès, relieved of all concern for his own person, practised extreme forms of resistance, finally working his way into the submarine base of the *Kriegsmarine* at Lorient dressed in a boiler suit, with a detached tenacity, as befits a scientist, for whom death was just a theoretically possible, neutral outcome. For, as Spinoza says, 'A free man thinks of nothing less than of death, and his wisdom is a meditation not of death but of life.'[6]

Canguilhem concludes: 'Cavaillès was resistant *by logic*.'

This 'by logic' contains the connection between philosophical rigour and the political prescription. It is not moral concern or, as we say nowadays, ethical discourse that have, it seems, produced the greatest figures of philosophy as resistance. The concept appears to have been a better guide on this matter than consciousness or spirituality – Canguilhem taunts those who, as philosophers of the individual, morality, consciousness, or even commitment, 'only speak so much about themselves because they alone can speak of their resistance, since it was so discreet.'[7]

In philosophy, we can prove that it is not necessary (at least in France) for the philosopher to be guided by moral consciousness and the Kantian categorical imperative in cases where choice and free will are abruptly called into action, in order to oppose dominant, ready-made opinion.

After all, the great philosopher who attests to a perilous act of resistance is certainly not Kant. It is rather Spinoza, the ultimate master of Cavaillès when, following the murder of the de Witt brothers, he wanted to put up a poster that stigmatised the *ultimi barbarorum*, the 'worst of barbarians'. It was an anecdote Canguilhem never grew tired of commenting on.

With Cavaillès, in the process of passing from Husserl to Spinoza – or equally with Albert Lautman who, on the basis of a staggering mastery of the mathematics of his time, attempted to found a modern Platonism – we are presented with the singular background of the exemplary resistant figures of French philosophy.

Both were shot by the Nazis. And it is no exaggeration to say that as a result of this the course of philosophy in France was enduringly altered. For, of this intimate connection between the radical mutation of twentieth-century mathematics and philosophy, there was, for a quarter of a century, to be almost no further mention in our country. Thus the Resistance would in fact have been both the sign of a relation between decision and abstract thought, and the transformation of this sign into an enigma, since those who were its symbolic bearers were killed in combat. In place of this came the Sartrean theory of commitment, which is evidently a *trompe l'oeil* assessment of that which was played out in the sequence of the Resistance.

But I can read even more in Canguilhem's formula: 'resistant by logic'. Other philosophical lessons.

First of all, I believe that this formula renders futile every attempt to assign the study of the Resistance to sociological or institutional representations. No group, no class, no social configuration or mental objective was behind the Resistance. And, for example, there is no consistent tale of 'Philosophers and the Resistance'. There was nothing in the course of this sequence which could have been described in terms of objective groups, be they 'workers' or 'philosophers'. This results from the fact that a Resistance figure 'by logic' obeys an axiom, or an injunction, which he formulates in his own name, and whose major consequences he lays out, without waiting to win over other people, in the objective group to which he belongs. Let us say that this resistance, proceeding by logic, is not an opinion. Rather it is a logical rupture with dominant and circulating opinions, just as Plato indicates, in the *Republic*, that the first stage of the rupture with opinion is mathematics, which after all clarifies the choice of Cavaillès and Lautman. But perhaps on this point I am under the influence of the Father figure. For it was very early on that my father introduced me to his own resistance as purely logical. From the moment that the country was invaded and subjugated by the Nazis, he said, there was nothing else for it than to resist. It was no more complicated than that. But then my father was a mathematician.

I shall thus posit that, detached from the consideration of sociological entities, as well as from the hazards of moral philosophy, the Resistance was neither a class phenomenon nor an ethical phenomenon.

Hence its importance for us. For the contemporary philosophical situation is one where, on the ruins of the doctrine of classes and class consciousness, attempts are made from all sides to restore the primacy of morality.

Grasped through its philosophical figures, the Resistance indicates almost blindly another path. The choice of political allegiance appears as one which is separated from the constraints of collective groups, and which falls within the competent realm of personal decisions. But, symmetrically, this choice is no longer subordinated to preexistent ethical maxims, and even less to a spiritual or juridical doctrine of human rights. The 'by logic' of Canguilhem must be understood as a double separation. First it separates itself from the 'by social necessity' that would dissolve choice into collective representations to be grasped through historical sociology. And second it separates itself from a pure moral imperative that would dissolve choice into doctrinal dispositions external to the situation concerned. In fact, choice has its intelligibility neither in the objective collective nor in a subjectivity of opinion. Its intelligibility is internal, in the sequential process of action, just as an axiom is intelligible only through the application of the theory that it supports.

Some believed for a time in setting up a great public debate on the transition from the thesis common to Gaullism and the PCF: 'all France was resistant', to the historiographic and sociological thesis: 'all France was Pétainist'. It is the method of this debate that is intellectually inadmissible, just as the two statements that it opposes are not false, but meaningless. For no genuine political sequence is representable in the universe of numbers and statistics.

In France, it is true that the State was the Pétainist puppet State, which had considerable consequences in terms of public opinion. And it is equally true that there were Resistance figures, therefore a Resistance, which also had considerable consequences. None of this is conceivable numerically. And primarily because the Resistance would never have had the least existence itself if, in order to exist, it had held out for an awareness of its own numbers, or for an assessment of its sociological role, or if it had been obliged to pronounce with certainty on the state of public opinion.

All resistance is a rupture with what is. And every rupture begins, for those engaged in it, through a rupture with oneself. The philosophers of the Resistance drew attention to this point, and to the fact that it existed in the realm of thought.

For this is the ultimate signification of the 'by logic' of Canguilhem. To tell it like it is, and to draw the consequences of this 'telling' situation, is in the first place, as much for an Auvergne peasant as for a philosopher, an operation of thought. It is this operation which, although totally natural and practical in its Real, refers neither to the objective analysis of social groups, nor to opinions that could have been formulated in advance. Those who did not resist, if we leave aside the clique of conscious collaborators, were quite simply those who did not want to tell the situation like it was, not even to themselves. It is no exaggeration to say that they did not think. What I mean by this is that they did not think according to the Real of the situation at the moment in question, that they rejected the fact that this Real was, for them personally, the bearer of a possibility for action, as is every Real when – according to the expression of Sylvain Lazarus that we shall come across later on – thought puts us in relation of it [*nous en fait rapport*].

When all is said and done, all resistance is a rupture in thought, through the declaration of what the situation is, and the foundation of a practical possibility opened up through this declaration.

Unlike what is often upheld this does not amount to believing that it is the risk, very serious indeed, which prevents a good many from resisting. It is on the contrary the non-thinking of the situation that prevents the risk, or the examination of possibles. Not to resist is not to think. Not to think is not *to risk risking*.

Cavaillès, Lautman, and a great many others who were by no means philosophers, only thought it important to tell the situation like it was, and therefore to risk that there were risks – and there are always a good many, great or small, when thought opens up possibles. That is why today, when to think the necessity of thinking the Real of the situation is rare – for the consensus held in such high esteem is the non-thinking politics of no alternative [*la non-pensée comme pensée unique*] – we can turn with gratitude towards the Resistance figures. For as Spinoza, Cavaillès' philosophical inspiration, says, 'Only free men are truly grateful one to the other.'[8]

Notes

1 Georges Canguilhem, *Vie et mort de Jean Cavaillès*, Paris: Allia, 1996.

2 Office de radiodiffusion-télévision française. *Trans.*

3 Canguilhem, *Vie et mort de Jean Cavaillès*, p. 37.

4 Jean Cavaillès, *Sur la logique et la théorie de la science*, Paris: Presses Universitaires de France, 1947.

5 Cited in Canguilhem, *Vie et mort de Jean Cavaillès*, p. 29.

6 Spinoza, *Ethics*, trans. Andrew Boyle, revised by G.H.R. Parkinson. London: Dent, 1993, IVP67.

7 Canguilhem, *Vie et mort de Jean Cavaillès*, p. 38.

8 Spinoza, *Ethics*, IVP71.

1

Against 'Political Philosophy'

One of the core demands of contemporary thought is to have done with 'political philosophy'. What is political philosophy? It is the programme which, holding politics – or, better still, the political – as an objective datum, or even invariant, of universal experience, accords philosophy the task of thinking it. Overall, philosophy's task would be to generate an analysis of the political and, *in fine*, quite obviously to submit this analysis to ethical norms. The philosopher would then have the triple advantage of being, first, the analyst and thinker of this brutal and confused objectivity which constitutes the empirical character of real instances of politics; second, the one who determines the principles of the good politics, of politics conforming to ethical demands; and, third, in order to meet these demands, the one exempt from militant involvement in any genuine political process. Whence the philosopher could keep the Real at arm's length indefinitely in the manner most dear to him: that of judgement.

The central operation of political philosophy thus conceived – which, admittedly, exemplifies what a certain 'philosophical' Pharisaism is capable of – is, first and foremost, to restore politics, not to the subjective reality of organised and militant processes – which, it must be said, are the only ones worthy of this name – but to the exercise of 'free judgement' in a public space where, ultimately, only opinions count.

A characteristic example of this gesture is Myriam Revault d'Allonnes' interpretation of the ideas of Hannah Arendt, whose achievements, impressive as they may be (notably her historicising analyses of imperialism), cannot be absolved of the innumerable 'political philosophies', shot through with the ethics of rights, which her work invokes.

Let us treat as our basic text the French edition of Hannah Arendt's lectures on Kant's political philosophy,[1] edited by Myriam Revault d'Allonnes, whose postface the editor revealingly entitles: 'The Courage of Judgement'.

What is 'politics' the name of, both in this postface as well as in the lectures themselves? And why is Kant the philosophical proper name summoned as guarantor for this understanding of the word 'politics'?

Within the configuration on offer to us here, what 'politics' is *not* the name of is in any case quite clear. 'Politics' is neither the name of a thought (if one admits that all thought, in the realm of its philosophical identification, is in one way or another bound to the theme of truth) nor the name of an action. I admit to being quite struck by this double negation. If politics is not a truth procedure touching the being of the collective in question, or even the construction and the animation of a new and singular collective, aiming for the control or transformation of what is, what can it be? I mean: what can it be *for philosophy*? Neither a determinant factor as far as the objectivity of situations is concerned, nor a militant agent in the seizure of their latent possibles, what does politics consist in?

The double negation is in any case indisputable. Hannah Arendt, for example, congratulates Kant for explaining 'how to take others into account, albeit without informing one how to combine with them in order to act'.[2] The perspective of the spectator is systematically privileged. Arendt justifies the fact that Kant had a 'boundless admiration' for the French Revolution as a phenomenon, or historical appearance, whilst nurturing 'a boundless opposition' to its revolutionary ventures and their actors. As a public spectacle the Revolution is admirable, while its militants are contemptible. From enthusiasm for the Revolution to abhorrence for Robespierre and Saint-Just: what must 'politics' mean for such a separation to come about?

Hannah Arendt does not hesitate, moreover, to push the characterisation to the point of registering an automatic contradiction between the judgement of the spectator and the maxim of the actor. She agrees with Kant's recognition of a 'clash between the principle according to which you should act and the principle according to which you judge'.[3]

One will demand to know at once if politics must therefore be established on the side of inactive judgement, or of the judgement which issues no maxims for action. And, if this is the case, what name can the maxim of public *action* lay claim to? But let's take things one step at a time.

What is certain is that the *subject* prescribed in the name of 'politics' will be called a 'world-spectator'. It is as if, let it be said in passing, the theatre were situated, not in relation to what authors, actors and directors do, but solely in relation to the audience.

In the very rigorous passage where Revault d'Allonnes sets about systematising the elements of the 'political way', one finds, in the following order:

- the particular, which is the phenomenal or evental assignation of politics;

- the faculty of judgement, which is a condition for the exercise of judgement, inasmuch as to judge requires the plurality of men, or the public space of opinion.

On this basis politics, whether in regard to a phenomenality without object, or in the realm of 'what happens', is the public exercise of a judgement.

Obviously, one will ask why politics would not exist in the realm of 'what happens' itself, as a thinkable *modification* of public space. Essentially Revault d'Allonnes wants to maintain this gap, within which political judgement is constructed, since politics, according to her reading, is under no circumstances the principle, the maxim or the prescription of a collective action aiming to transform the plural situation (or public space) itself.

It is clear, then, that what politics is the name of concerns, and only concerns, *public opinion*. What is overtly eradicated here is the militant identification of politics (which, for me, is nevertheless the *only* identification which can ally politics and thought).

As soon as 'politics' finds its sole rightful place in public opinion it goes without saying that the theme of truth is excluded from it. For Hannah Arendt, reader of Kant, as for Revault d'Allonnes, reader of both Kant and Arendt, politics is anything but a truth procedure. Revault d'Allonnes isolates what she calls 'the antagonism of truth and opinion, of the mode of philosophical life and the mode of political life',[4] as the matrix of Arendt's thought.

One will note in passing that, long before being Arendtian or Kantian, the theme of the irreducible opposition of truth and opinion is Platonic; as is, equally, the idea of a philosophical monopoly of truth – an idea surrounded by the connection between truth and the 'philosophical life' (which, incidentally, makes one wonder quite what a 'philosophical life' might be).

But what is *not* Platonic is the idea that politics (the 'political life') is forever devoted to opinion, forever disjoined from all truth. We know what this idea amounts to: sophistry. And it certainly seems to be the case that what Arendt and Revault d'Allonnes mean by 'politics'– and I will return to this question presently – is sophistry in the modern sense of the word, that is to say a sophistry dedicated to the promotion of an entirely particular politics. In other words: parliamentary politics.

In fact, what we have here is an orientation of thought whose tradition has been established ever since the Greeks, and which disqualifies, in matters of politics, the theme of truth as univocal and tyrannical. Everyone knows that there is a precious 'freedom of opinion', whereas the 'freedom of truth' remains in doubt. In the lengthy succession of banalities pronounced on the 'dogmatic', 'abstract' and 'constrained' character of the idea of truth – banalities forever invested in defence of political regimes whose (generally economic) authority to exercise power is concealed behind the 'freedom of opinion' – Arendt declares that 'every truth "unequivocally demands recognition and refuses debate to the extent that debate constitutes the very essence of political life"'.[5]

This banality contains at least two inaccuracies.

First of all, a singular truth is always the result of a complex process in which debate is decisive. Science itself began – with mathematics – with the radical renunciation of every principle of authority. Scientific statements are *accurately* exposed in their entirety to general criticism, independently of the subject of enunciation, and in accordance with explicit norms that are accessible by right to whomsoever takes the trouble to grasp them. A truth, whose normative construction gains resolute approval in the process of being shared, is perhaps the only thing that 'demands' nothing at all. The antinomy of truth and debate is a bad joke.

Except, of course, if one deems it absolutely necessary to assert *special rights* for falsity and for lying. In this case, it would instead be necessary to say the following: debate, *which confers rights without norms upon falsity and lying,* constitutes the very essence of politics. But what Revault d'Allonnes calls 'the courage of judgement' is more like the laziness of those who are sheltered from every norm and see their errors or their lies protected by right.

So, in supposing that 'debate' is the essence of politics, must we conclude that antagonism exists between this 'debate' and all truth? It all depends on what the debate is aimed at. Here we re-encounter the impasses of the disjunction between 'judgement' and 'maxim of action'. It is indeed clear that, apart from those who believe that saloon bar philosophy or conversations between friends constitute 'the very essence of political life', debate is political only to the extent that it crystallises in a decision. The question of a possible political truth must then be examined not only on the basis of 'debate' – which, in isolation, turns 'politics' into mere passive commentary on current affairs, a kind of collective extension of reading newspapers – but in the complex process which allies debate with decision, or which concentrates debate in *political statements* in whose name one or more interventions are possible. Even public parliamentary debate is punctuated by that minimalist form of general intervention that is the vote. It's certainly true that voting has little to do with truth. If our knowledge of planetary motion relied solely on suffrage as its protocol of legitimation, we would still inhabit a geocentric universe. But this is to judge the particular procedure of voting, not the possible generic bond between public debate and truth. Here again, Arendt and Revault d'Allonnes fall under the jurisdiction of a particular politics, one that presents the false articulation of opinions and governmental power from the standpoint of voting. Voting is so obviously foreign to all truth (even in the sense of conservative opinion: it brings Hitler to power just as easily as Pétain or the Algerian Islamists) that, for those who wish to uphold this figure of 'democracy' philosophically, it is *necessary* to sever 'the' political from the protocols of decision, to reduce it to the judgement of the spectator, and to think of debate as a plural confrontation of opinions without truth.

Speaking of 'the' political here masks the philosophical defence of *a* politics, which merely confirms my belief that every philosophy is conditioned by a *real* politics.

It is interesting to note in this respect how the defence of parliamentarianism, expressed through philosophemes, is indeed able to justify itself by means of Kant's distinctions. This is what makes the reading of Arendt and Revault d'Allonnes a real contemporary philosophical exercise. What do the sovereignty of the spectator and the absolute primacy of debate actually mean? That 'politics' is the name of what concerns, not determinant judgement, but reflexive judgement. In fact it is not a question of laying down maxims for action, or of analysing objective configurations. Politics is to be found in a public judgement which states whether *this* – which is not an object, but an appearing, a taking-place – pleases me or displeases me, and is exercised in the debate of such judgements. Such a position ultimately refers politics back to the public plurality of opinions, a plurality which parliamentarianism claims to connect to the State through the plurality of parties.

'Pluralism', which is another name for parliamentarianism (in propaganda successive instances of this sort of politics are generally *the same*), thereby finds itself invested with a transcendental legitimacy. Revault d'Allonnes will argue that the entire effort is to 'rehabilitate opinion, to restore its specific dignity while confronting the primacy of rational truth'.[6]

Incidentally, I wonder where Revault d'Allonnes can see today, in the field of politics, a 'primacy of rational truth'. Who shares this 'primacy'? It is obvious that we are living through the unconditioned primacy of opinions. Even in philosophy the prevailing tendencies, all of which are post-Nietzschean and anti-Platonist, have denigrated 'rational truth', equating it with 'metaphysics'. In reality, as ever, truths are rare and precarious, their action restricted. If it's a battle for rehabilitation, it is certainly the theme of truth – against the hegemony of 'freedom of opinion' – which is due to benefit, through the support of some real truths, from the overturning of philosophical relativism and the critique of capitalist-parliamentarianism.

In the transcendental promotion of the pluralism of opinions, Arendt and Revault d'Allonnes obviously come up against an essential problem: how can the innate plurality of men and opinions be allied with the *exercise* of judgement? According to which procedures are the objectivity of the multiple and the reflexive subjectivity of judgement on the phenomenality of this multiple articulated?

This question presents a twofold difficulty, and both Arendt and Revault d'Allonnes excel in unfolding its duplicity.

1. If politics constitutes the instance of judgement over an *unbound* phenomenal multiplicity – i.e. a multiplicity undetermined in its objective form – what stable faculty is responsible for forming opinions which bind this diversity, or give a verdict on the unbinding? This is the question of the *formation* of opinions.

2. If nothing exists *apart from* the public space of opinions, how can these opinions enter into the debate? And what rule

drives this debate in a way which might suppose that the resulting judgement has any significance, even if only the averting of disaster? This is the question of good and evil, or of the value of the adjective 'democratic' (providing 'democracy' names the freedom to form and discuss opinions).

Let us call 'community' plurality as such; the being-together, or in-common, of the plurality of men. Let us call 'common sense' the resource of judgement *directly bound to this plurality*. Arendt's formula is then the following: 'The criterion is communicability, and the standard of deciding about it is common sense.'[7]

One might object, as so often happens with any doctrine of the 'faculties', that all we have done here is gone round in circles by providing the solution to the problem in name only. 'Communicability' suggests that the plurality of opinions is sufficiently wide-ranging to accommodate difference. And yet everyone knows from experience that this is inaccurate, and that there is no place for debating *genuinely* alternative opinions, which at best are subject to dispute. With 'common sense' one provides a norm that in actual fact is transcendent, because it suggests, not only plurality, but a subjective unity of this plurality, at least in principle. This concession to the One undoes the radicality of the multiple, which had allegedly been guaranteed. It opens the way for a doctrine of *consensus*, which is in effect the dominant ideology of contemporary parliamentary States.

Revault d'Allonnes refines Arendt's analysis a great deal, and this is undoubtedly her principal contribution. She does so in three statements:

1. 'Men are political beings because they exist in the plural. This plurality is not an obstacle to judgement, but its very

condition. Opinion is formed as the original exercise of "sharing the world with others".[8] One recognises what is at stake in this attempt: to assign the formation of opinions to the plural *itself*, to make it the immediate subjectification of being-together. The price paid for this move is a severe restriction as to what an opinion is – let's be clear: as to what a politically justified opinion is (I won't go so far as to say a 'politically correct' one ...). For this is an opinion which at least bears a trace of its protocol of formation, and which therefore *remains homogeneous to the persistence of being-together, or of the share [partage]*. Hence the fact that an anti-Semitic opinion, for example, is not regarded as a political opinion, and Nazism is not viewed as a politics. Alas, contemporary thought will not advance one bit without the courage to think that Nazism was a politics. A criminal politics, but a politics, of which 'Jew' was one of the categories. For fighting against a politics in the name of a necessary conformity of opinions grounded in being-together – as if what was being contested wasn't a politics, or even an opinion – is exactly what made for the unfathomably weak (and ongoing) manner in which the Western powers have dealt with Nazism.

2. Common sense, which is sense of the in-common, is the norm to the extent that it distributes the critical plurality of opinions in accordance with the discernment of good and evil. This discernment is the very ground [*fond*] of the in-common, and is the ultimate condition for thought: 'the power of thought is bound to the capacity to distinguish good from evil'.[9] In this case, we are faced with the attempt to prop up politics with ethics through the decidedly inexhaustible resources of the in-common. Ultimately, the norm that regulates the debating of opinions is the transcendental evidence of the good/evil distinction with respect to the in-common. One is tempted to

object that, in Kantian guise, we have reverted to the universally grounded transcendence of the good as the ultimate guarantee of political judgement. To which Revault d'Allonnes responds:

3. In the discernment of good and evil, the apperception of evil comes first. For evil is precisely what puts the in-common, or the share, in question. One sees here the opening of a theme dear to Revault d'Allonnes: radical evil. Political judgement is first and foremost resistance to evil. To judge is 'to attempt to resist impending evil in fear and trembling'.[10] I have already said what I think of this doctrine in my little book *Ethics*. I believe it to be inescapably theological and, moreover, politically inoperative. For every real figure of evil is presented, not as a fanatical non-opinion undermining being-together, but on the contrary as *a politics* aiming to ground *authentic* being-together. No 'common sense' can counter it; only *another politics* can do so. For all that, one will recognise in the reduction of political judgement to pure negation ('resisting evil') what has always been said about parliamentary democracies: that, while admittedly not good, they were 'the least bad' alternative.

Ultimately, the entire effort of Revault d'Allonnes is to equip the in-common with an immanent power, with a 'perseverance in being', similar to the Spinozist ontology of her political philosophy. Judgement must be adequate to this power, which means that it simply declares that what is, is good: the plurality of men devoted to being-together. More precisely, it conceives evil as lack of being (or of power) through the negative will to mutilate the common, or the community. Politics pronounces publicly the negation of this negation. Against negative will, it reaffirms the being which grounds its judgement: the power of the common.

To put it synthetically, politics according to Arendt and Revault d'Allonnes might then be defined as the name of those judgements which, regulated by the share of the common, resist evil, i.e. the destruction of this share.

Still proceeding synthetically, and since we have been 'politically' invited to debate, I will make five objections.

1. The 'ontological' characterisation of the political on the basis of plurality, or being-together, is certainly much too broad. Revault d'Allonnes is aware of this, which confirms why in this case it's a matter of an 'extension' of the concept of the political. To my mind, this extension ruins the singularity of what must be thought here. Plurality is the ground of being in general. It is, in terms of multiplicity bound or unbound, involved in every procedure of thought, regardless of type. I have already said that science is itself exposed from the outset to the common, to being-together, to debate. The poem is equally unthinkable without its mode of address. This co-presence of the multiple in every exercise of thought is, from Plato to Lacan, named the power of the Other. And, of course, politics also falls within this domain. But it must be singularised far downstream from the authority of the in-common, or the Other. It involves at least four multiplicities: the infinity of situations; the superpower of the State; evental ruptures; militant prescriptions, statements and practices (the complete process of the definition of politics will be sketched out at the end of this book).

Now, each one of these multiplicities is itself singular, and relates to a distinct ontological investigation. This is what I call establishing the *numericality* of a truth procedure. There is no simple plurality, there is plurality of pluralities, seized and torn asunder in the sequence which runs from the situation (whose infinity is the stake peculiar to all politics) to the formula for equality (the empty sign 'equals'), via the infinity of the State (always superior to that of the situation, but errantly so) and the evental distancing of this superiority through the event. Only the complexity of this cycle explains how there can be political judgements *as judgements of truth*, as opposed to mere opinions. For the subject of these judgements – unlike the transcendental subject supposedly behind the 'common sense' of Arendt – is *constituted* through the political process itself. And this constitution is precisely what wrests it from the regime of opinion.

2. Revault d'Allonnes is right to highlight the particular, the pure phenomenon of the taking-place. But in my view she brings about a gradual transcendental reduction in this particularity. The supposed existence of a generic faculty for the discernment of evil means that, for her, the matrix of 'political' judgement is ultimately invariable. Phenomenal particularity is only the *material* for a judgement whose maxim is fixed and which would take the following form: 'Always declare yourself in favour of the persistence of the share of the in-common.' This explains why her vision of politics is in the last resort *conservative*. Without the menace of radical evil, judgement is not absolutely requisite. In order to liven things up a bit, one shall say of course that evil is always impending. But how can we ground this imminence transcendentally, other than through some sinful tendency of human nature vis-à-vis the in-common? One sees here the fundamental reason why it is so important for these conceptions to maintain that 'the Beast is always lurking', that it stirs in each of us, and so on. Without this everlasting latency of the Beast, politics doesn't even have reason to exist.

In order to hold firm to the particular, or the singular, we must set out on an entirely different path. First, we must maintain that the inception of a politics – of its statements, prescriptions, judgements and practices – is always located in the absolute singularity of an event. Second, that a politics only exists within a sequence, that is to say, to the extent that what the event is 'capable' of is deployed in an act of truth. Finally, that what counts is never the plurality of opinions regulated by a common norm, but the plurality of instances of politics [*des politiques*] which have *no* common norm, since the subjects they induce are different.

Incidentally, one will reject the expression '*the* political', which precisely suggests a specific faculty, a common sense. There are only plural instances of politics, irreducible to one another, and which do not comprise any homogeneous history.

3. Every consensual vision of politics will be opposed. An event is never shared, even if the truth we gather from it is universal, because its recognition *as event* is simply at one with the political decision. A politics is a hazardous, militant and always partially undivided fidelity to evental singularity under a solely self-authorising prescription. The universality of political truth that results from such a fidelity is itself legible, like all truth, only retroactively, in the form of a knowledge. Of course, the point from which a politics can be thought – which permits, even after the event, the seizure of its truth – is that of its actors, and not its spectators. It is through Saint-Just and Robespierre that you enter into this singular truth unleashed by the French Revolution, and on the basis of which you form a knowledge, and not through Kant or François Furet.[11]

4. Since opinions do not refer to any underlying transcendental figure, the question of their formation and debate remains

entirely unresolved. We must maintain that every opinion actually *conforms* to a mode of politics, to a politics. Real plurality is characteristic of instances of politics; the plurality of opinions is only the referent of a particular politics (parliamentarianism).

Therefore it can be said that Arendt's configuration, conceived as 'philosophical opinion', obviously conforms to the parliamentary mode of politics.

5. The essence of politics is not the plurality of opinions. It is the prescription of a possibility in rupture with what exists. Of course, the exercise or the test of this prescription and the statements it commands – all of which is authorised by a faded event – goes by way of debates. But not exclusively. More important still are the declarations, interventions and organisations.

Indeed, if the political prescription is not explicit, opinions and debates inevitably fall under the invisible yoke of an implicit, or masked, prescription. And we know what draws support from every masked prescription: the State, and the instances of politics articulated around it.

Presenting itself as the philosophy of a politics of plurality, of the resistance to evil and the courage of judgement, this very peculiar neo-Kantianism is no less than a philosopheme suited to the prescriptions which sustain the parliamentary State.

This is why placing philosophy under condition of emancipatory politics requires a break with 'political philosophy' in Arendt's sense; it requires us to begin from the beginning, from the recognition that politics itself is, in its being, in its doing, a thought.

Prior to any philosophical capture, but serving as its condition, this is the central motif of what Sylvain Lazarus elaborates under the name 'intellectuality of politics'.

Notes

1 Hannah Arendt, *Juger. Sur la philosophie politique de Kant*, trans. and ed. Myriam Revault d'Allonnes. Paris: Seuil, 1991. [*Lectures on Kant's Political Philosophy*, ed. Ronald Beiner. Chicago: University of Chicago Press, 1982.]

2 Ibid., p. 73 [p. 44; translation modified].

3 Ibid., p. 79 [p. 48].

4 Ibid., p. 237.

5 Ibid.

6 Ibid.

7 Ibid., p. 108 [p. 69].

8 I have been unable to locate this reference. *Trans.*

9 Ibid., p. 227.

10 Ibid., p. 243.

11 François Furet, 1927–97. French revisionist historiographer and professor at the Ecole Pratique des Hautes Études. *Trans.*

Politics as Thought:
The Work of Sylvain Lazarus[1]

a) A Foundation

Sylvain Lazarus, who for a long time was content to act as an exemplary political leader and thinker in the realm of politics itself, finally published in 1996 a primary synthesis of his conceptions in a book entitled *The Anthropology of the Name*.[2] It is no exaggeration to say that, today, philosophers cannot attempt any seizure of politics as thought without studying this book, which is – that most rare of things – a foundational book in a three-fold sense.

1. The foundation of a discipline: the anthropology of the name. This discipline is *established* in its categories and statements; *vouchsafed* in its protocols (the inquests of worker anthropology conducted in – among others – French, Chinese, German and Polish factories, and inquests into the modes of existence of politics); *localised* through its disjunction from other real or possible anthropologies, namely post-Marxist dialectical anthropology and post-positivist structural anthropology; and subjectively *legitimated* through the evental occurrence which

punctuated its guiding problem. In this respect, the whole of Lazarus' first chapter, 'Itinerary and Categories', grounds the question: how can we think politics in the aftermath of May '68?

2. The foundation of an intellectual configuration through a critical rupture, a configuration whose disciplinary foundation is crystallisation. This configuration retroactively designates another figure of intellectuality, both dominant and outdated; namely, historicist, classist, dialectical or positivist thought (Lazarus demonstrates the equivalence of these terms). In breaking with positivist historicism, the central characteristic of the anthropology of the name is to authorise a thought of subjectivity which is strictly subjective, without passing through any type of objective mediation. More fundamentally still, it eliminates the category of the object. The whole problem is to think thought *as thought* and not as object; or again, to think that which is thought in thought, and not 'that which' (the object) thought thinks.

3. The foundation of a new system of conditions for philosophy. The anthropology of the name is by no means a philosophical discipline. To adopt the terminology of Lazarus, each register of thought entails the simple name of that which is thought within it, and such thought is a 'relation' [*rapport*] of this name.

The strangeness of the expression 'relation of' is the result of Lazarus' essential determination never to lapse into a definition of thought formulated on the basis of its supposed object(s). That which is thought in thought must be thinkable apart from the (positivist) form of the object. One will thus say that thought, inasmuch as it is thinkable, is a 'relation' of that which is thought in it, and which has no objectal status. 'Relation of' is clearly opposed to 'relation to'. Thought is not a relation *to* the object, it is an *internal* relation of its Real, which taken 'in itself' remains indistinct, since it is presented only through the identification of a singular thought.

Now, for Lazarus, there are three registers of 'subjectifying' thought, of the thought which *can* concern itself with the think-ability of thought itself. First there is history, whereby thought is a relation of the State. Second there is the anthropology of the name, which declares that thought is a relation of the Real. And last there is philosophy, whose constitutive statement is that thought is a relation of thought.

We shall say then that philosophy is put to the test by the anthropology of the name inasmuch as the effects of the latter affect the interiority of thought itself. What is a philosophy which is potentially contemporaneous with the anthropology of the name, and no longer with dialectical and positivist anthropolo-gies? How can a philosophy be established within a theory of the *objectless* subject, while holding firmly to the demands of rationalism, i.e. of materialism?

b) Names

First of all, we need to ask why Lazarus' undertaking invokes the name in its very title. What is a name? This question is only fully resolved at the end of the analysis. But it is equally its point of departure.

In an initial sense, the name is nothing other than the Real, and this is why it cannot have a definition: the Real is always indistinct, being identifiable only as a 'relation of' constitutive of thought. Lazarus writes: 'I call "name" that which is thought in thought and which is not given in itself or directly'.[3] One will also say: the (simple) name is that which 'opens up' thought, and which must be maintained throughout the investigation, without ever being 'objectified' by a definition or a referent. 'The simple name is a word that opens up a field for thought: for example, politics. Every word is not a simple name. But to maintain the presence of a simple name throughout the investigation … prohibits and prevents every metalanguage and every diversion.'[4] To prohibit metalanguage (a point on which Lazarus communicates equally well with Wittgenstein and Lacan) ultimately comes down to upholding an ethic of names, and in two directions:

- Not to objectify the name, not to wrest it from its subjective irruption, which is its sole means of opening up thought. In the final analysis, this means: *not to name the name*, safeguarding its status as unnameable name. In this way we avoid advancing towards any definition or nomination, either of thought (it is, Lazarus says, 'the first of simple names'[5]), or of revolutionary politics, or of the word 'worker', etc.
- Not to abandon the name either, or to refer it to something other than itself, or again: not to forget that the names are distinct, that 'what each name deals with cannot be shared with what is dealt with by another name'.[6] One abandons the name each time one pretends to inscribe it within a totality. Why? Because all thinking in terms of totality pretends to think 'at the same time' (Lazarus says: to co-think) that which is opened up in thought by the name, and the way in which the name is relative to the totality. For example, one might claim that the thinking of politics refers back to the historical totality, or to society as a composite totality. In this case, Lazarus says, the name is *sacrificed*. This means that what the name opens up to thought, no longer being thinkable on its

own terms (politics ceasing to be thinkable through politics),
is no longer the split index of the *singularity* of a thought, but
rather a notion which circulates in heterogeneous fields, i.e.
a concept. For 'concepts, not names, are exportable'.[7]

Ultimately the ethic of names, as the sole means of preventing thought from overbalancing into exteriority (thought being
rendered on the basis of its objects), paradoxically consists in
opposing the name to nomination. This is perhaps the point
where Lazarus' wish to maintain, from start to finish, a path
of interiority wherein the name (but not the sacrificed one)
persists without ever becoming a concept is the most strained.
Let us quote the key passage: 'Thought can think its own
thought, but cannot give itself a name, owing to the impossibility of a nomination of interiority.'[8] If, indeed, thought were
related to itself through a nomination of what it is, it would
constitute an object for itself. The name must therefore open
up thought, inhabit it from start to finish, and not proceed to
any type of nomination, whether with respect to itself or the
Real whose split index it is. This is a preliminary condition for
declaring that 'in the formula "anthropology of the name",
the name designates the will to apprehend singularity without
making it disappear'.[9]

An example is in order here. Let us suppose that the proper
name of that which took place in France between 1792 and 1794
is 'revolutionary politics'. For the sake of thinking the thought
that identifies that which took place (and whose principal reference, for Lazarus, is Saint-Just) there will neither be a definition
of politics nor a practicable nomination of the name 'political
revolutionary'. It will no longer be possible to refer the name
'revolutionary politics' to a composite totality, such as 'French
society in 1792', or 'politics of the ascendant bourgeoisie', etc.

These attempts, prevalent in historiography, sacrifice the name because they rule out the apprehension, in the realm of interiority, of the thought of Saint-Just as a political singularity. In order to succeed rationally in this task, the name must be subtracted from any direct conceptualisation (thought cannot be a thought *of* the name, or a thought of revolutionary politics as such), at the same time as the name is well and truly that which is thought in the thought of Saint-Just.

The objections are predictable: if, in *The Anthropology of the Name*, the name is never presented as an object of thought, if it is unnameable in this case, what does anthropology think? Certainly, it's a question of that which is thought in thought, and quite generally in the thought of 'people' [*gens*] (the first statement of *The Anthropology of the Name* is: 'people think'). There is anthropology 'from the moment when the question which is posed is that of knowing if thought is thinkable'.[10] Fine. But if the thinkability of thought encounters the name as being both the principal index of the singularity of a thought *and* the unnameable or the indefinable of this singularity, are we not in an impasse? The systematic subtlety of Lazarus' undertaking consists in establishing that we are not. The thinkability of thought will be distributed 'through' the name – but without naming it – courtesy of three fundamental inventions.

1. Of course, the name has no name or definition. But this means that it is not a name *of what exists*. If this were the case, we could identify the name through the reality that it designates, and we would take leave of interiority. In fact, as is particularly clear with the name 'politics' (but this is not the only case), a name is always the index of an overbalancing [*bascule*] of what exists into what *can* exist, or from the known towards the unknown. Thought exists only to the extent that this overbalancing exists,

otherwise the positivist notion of knowledge would suffice. To say 'people think' is to say that they are capable, under a name, of prescribing a possible that is irreducible to the repetition or the continuation of what exists. Consequently, the essence of the name, in *The Anthropology of the Name*, is not descriptive: it is *prescriptive*. When that which is thought in a mode of thought is the Real, it is a name insomuch as its being is not what is, but what can be. In other words, it is neither a necessary determination nor an absolute contingency. One will therefore posit that the unnameable 'essence' of the name is that which conjoins a possible and a prescription.

2. Now, every prescription is given in statements, and these statements are thinkable through the categories they convey. Here we shall strenuously distinguish 'category' from 'concept'. The concept is always a sacrifice of the name as singularity. A category is that which only exists within the singular interiority of a thought. It is what organises the intellectuality of a prescription. For example, for Saint-Just, the categories of virtue or corruption are given in prescriptive statements about the situation, and these statements in turn vouchsafe the existence of the name (revolutionary politics) as a singular thought, without so much as naming or defining it. 'I call *category*, in respect of phenomena of consciousness, whatever has existence only within singularity. A category can be named and identified, but not defined; for in the field of the phenomena of consciousness every definition requires the concept, the object, and leads to science as an exclusive model.'[11] The name is unnameable, and in this sense the pure historicity of singularity, its 'there is' as such, remains unthinkable. But the categories of the name, or the intellectuality of its prescriptive nature, are nameable, and therefore authorise a thought of this intellectuality. This thought will

proceed in interiority, because it will assign the category to nothing other than singularity and, never proceeding by way of definitions, will provide it with no other extension than the seizure of the name's prescriptive nature.

3. Finally, the name possesses places. 'The name exists, by which we understand: singularity exists; but it cannot be named and is only seized through its emergent *places*.'[12] Every name is deployed in its places, or through the materiality of the prescription. By way of example, we might ask *where* – in the form of situations bearing a possible that will have been established by a prescription – we should seek verification of statements of the unnameable name 'revolutionary politics' between 1792 and 1794. The answer is patently obvious: in the Convention, its debates and decisions; in the gatherings of the *sansculottes*; and in the army of Year II. But one will ask: how? By citing these factual data, doesn't one cause the name to lapse into a multiple system of objective referents? Not at all. For these places, named but indefinable, are rigorously coextensive with the singularity of the name. They are themselves prescriptions, which localise the name within a multiplicity, a multiplicity that has the essential property of *remaining homogeneous to the subjectivity that it localises*. Let us quote a crucial passage:

> The places of a name are an existential modality of the subjective. As far as the unnameable name of a politics is concerned – think of the given identification of revolutionary politics – its places … are all homogeneous because they are subjective, and subjective because they are prescriptive. Moreover, they are prescriptive because they stem from a thought of politics whose essential movement is that of a separation which inscribes the possible as a rational and practicable character of this separation.[13]

If you consider the Convention or the gatherings of the *sans-culottes* as the objective results of a nameable and definable revolutionary politics, you inhabit a dialectic of the subjective and the objective which institutes *heterogeneous multiplicities*. You act as though it were possible to 'co-think' the mental (the ideas and convictions of revolutionaries) and the material (the Convention, etc.). In so doing, you sacrifice the name (which disappears as singularity within the dialectical totality), and you ultimately cause politics as thought to disappear: thought becomes unthinkable. If, on the other hand, you consider the Convention and other material instances as places of the name – in other words, as processes which are themselves prescriptive, and which share the same fabric as political subjectivity – then you retain the name and, establishing the investigation in a *homogeneous multiplicity*, you are able to think thought in interiority. That the homogeneous multiplicity of places is rigorously coextensive with the prescriptive nature of the name is proved by the fact that, as soon as a place disappears, the general political configuration is terminated. For example, as soon as the Soviets, which are one of the places of Bolshevik politics, disappear (thus from autumn 1917), the Bolshevik political mode, whose thought Lenin names, ceases to exist.

In equipping himself with the prescription, categories of the name and the places of the name, Lazarus succeeds in thinking the singularity of a thought without referring it to objective referents and without dissolving it within a totality. It appears, then, that singularity is always prescriptive and that, like every prescription, it is sequential and precarious. For 'to think is to prescribe thought',[14] which happens occasionally – rarely – for a time. How might this precariousness 'forever' *interest* thought? We are entering into the difficult section of *The Anthropology of the Name* that confronts the question of Time.

c) Against Time

Let us say at once, as his thesis is radical and surprising, that Lazarus' rational conviction is that it is only possible to think the singularity of a thought by *evacuating time*. One section of Chapter IV bears the audacious title: 'Abolition of the Category of Time'.[15]

This point is demonstrated in two ways. First, through the discussion of Marc Bloch's work, for whom time is the 'element', or the plasma, of history. And, more directly, through the doctrine of the possible.

The first point, detailed and subtle, centres – for the philosopher that I am – on the question of knowing how to 'leave' Hegel. For Hegel, Lazarus remarks, time is purely subjective and sides with the Absolute Idea. Or again: time is the being-there of the concept as subjectified presentation of the Absolute. The critique of Hegelian idealism can therefore be enacted in two ways, not just one. The first, which is the more classical (and classist), consists in desubjectifying time, in introducing historical time as material and objective time, while maintaining it as a dimension of historical consciousness, which is consciousness *of* objective temporality. One then enters into the regime of heterogeneous multiplicity, wherein time circulates between the material and the mental, between the objective and the subjective. Although he explores the limits of this idea (which makes him a great thinker of history), this is indeed the position maintained by Marc Bloch. As Lazarus remarks, with Bloch 'time remains a circulating notion because it offers a space of circulation: men in time from the material perspective and from the subjective perspective'.[16] But then, as is always the case when one sets out from a notion that circulates in the heterogeneous realm, one will not succeed in thinking the singularity of a thought. For singularity is attached to the maintenance of the univocity of the name, and if you have a circulating notion then it is by definition a *polysemic unity*. This is one of Lazarus' constant themes: if the aim is to think a thought as singularity, you cannot sacrifice the univocity of the name through the (hermeneutic) appeal to nominal polysemic unities, which establish heterogeneous multiplicities. Time remains, with Bloch, one such unity, simultaneously interpretable from the objective and subjective sides. We must therefore leave Hegel via a different route from Bloch. Not by distributing time through the heterogeneous multiplicity of the objective and the subjective (this is also Marx's position, since for him it is on the basis of time that [objective] social being determines consciousness) but through the abolition of all (polysemic) uniqueness of time, or of any reference to the category of time, in favour of the name and the places of the name. This strictly subjective approach is what 'saves' an aspect of Hegel. But it does so whilst preventing thinkable singularities from being subsumed by the idealist Absolute. Lazarus concludes, in his dense style: 'In our approach, the name permits the abolition of the category of time. The name does not subsume time, it proceeds to its nominal abolition through the passage to uniqueness, followed by the attribution of multiplicity to the movement which proceeds from the name to the place of the name.'[17]

The approach to the question of time through the category of the possible is more fundamental still. We know, in fact, that every singularity is prescriptive. Now, the prescription is a thought of what can be with respect to what is, and it is prescription which is borne along by the statements of thought: 'Statements are prescriptions. They are prescriptive declarations of what "there is".... There is only a thought of statements.'[18] The category of the possible 'bears' the statement as the elementary unity of a singular thought. But how can we think the possible without reintroducing the category of time? For Lazarus, the possible is by no means a category of the future, and at the heart of his thought one finds a de-temporalisation of the possible. The possible, in being homogeneous to 'what there is', is not the substance or nature of what can come about. It is not an external given, a heterogeneous entity which would only be presented through the polysemic unity of time. The possible is 'that which permits thought to think the relation between what can come about and what is'.[19] Now, this relation can take two forms which set *The Anthropology of the Name* apart from any positivist sociology, as well as from any temporalised history: 'either the relation is prescriptive, a rupture between what can come about and what is; or it is descriptive, allowing us to infer what will come about on the basis of what is'.[20] Only the descriptive relation requires time, because it makes the possible into an attribute of what will come about. In the case of a thought of singularity as prescription, *what happens does not cancel out the fact that what could have taken place lies behind the organ-isation of the prescriptive statements.* Seized in interiority, the possible remains as the subjective content governing what takes place, whatever the 'nature' of this taking-place might be. Let us quote the conclusion, which is really crucial:

> The possible is a subjective category [*catégorie en subjectivité*] which problematises the approach of what can be with respect to what is, in the future as well as in the past. What can be, in comparison to what is, traverses the future, the past and the present in equal measure. Not qua unrepeatable, but as follows: what takes place does not abolish its preceding subjective contents. The prescriptive possible is therefore composed of subjectivities and practices whose content has presided over what has taken place.[21]

This clarifies why one is able to think the singularity of a thought within a strictly prescriptive and self-constituting realm of interiority, both rationally (through the category of the name and places of the name), and without having to immerse it in the heterogeneity of time: what has taken place is thinkable, both as a precarious singularity restricted by dates ('the work of identification ... is achieved through the delimitation of the sequence and its dating'[22]) and as indifferent to time. To think a singularity does indeed determine it, in the words of Thucydides, in the guise of an 'eternal acquisition'.

d) The Historical Modes of Politics

In no way whatsoever does *The Anthropology of the Name* claim to carry out an inventory and classification of names (this would make its enterprise structural). The investigation is carried out singularity by singularity, through the passage from the word to the category whose name is an unnameable singularity (recall that a category grasps the prescriptive content of the statements of a singular thought). As Lazarus says:

> we must make sure that the passage from the word – which is simply linguistic – to the category is possible through the path of intellectuality, then through the thinkable, and finally through the relation to the Real. The condition for this development is that the word opens onto a name that is deployed in its places.[23]

Lazarus' book enacts this approach by setting out from two words, considered as simple names: the word 'politics' and the word 'worker'. How, in these two cases, is the passage to the category made, and what is the category? Then, once the category has been identified (and named), what are the identified 'cases' of singularities (of unnameable names) whose category is the category, and what are the places of these cases?

In order to delimit our abstraction, let us provide some immediate examples and results.

The category that corresponds to the name 'politics' is that of the *historical mode of politics*, which supports the seizure of the intellectuality of a politics, which is what Lazarus calls 'the relation of a politics to its thought'. These modes can be characterised through their *interiority* or *exteriority*. They are 'interior' when the multiplicity of their places remains a homogeneous (subjective, prescribed) multiplicity. They are 'exterior' when the multiplicity is heterogeneous, and when the name is presented as having only a single place: the State.

The interior modes identified by Lazarus (but the list never claims to be closed) are the following:

- the revolutionary mode (Saint-Just), of which we have already spoken, and whose sequence is 1792–94;
- the classist mode (Marx), in which history is the subjectified category of politics, whose places are the working-class movements, and whose sequence runs from 1848 (*Manifesto of the Communist Party*) to 1871 (the Paris Commune);
- the Bolshevik mode (Lenin), identified by the conditioning of politics (the proletarian political capacity must identify its own conditions, the party crystallises this imperative), whose places are the party and the Soviets, and whose sequence runs from 1902 (*What is to be done?*) to 1917 (disappearance of the Soviets and 'statification' of the party);
- the dialectical mode (Mao Tse-tung), identified through the dialectical laws of politics, as distinct from the 'laws' of history, which permit a mobile treatment of situations and conjunctures

– a mode whose places are those of the revolutionary war
(the party, the army, the united front), and whose sequence
runs from 1928 (*Why Can China's Red Political Power Exist?*[24])
to 1958 (the outcome of the Korean War).

The exterior modes are:

- the parliamentary mode in France, whose sequence began after
  1968, and whose singularity is fastened to the functional and
  consensual determination of the State (hence the fact that parties
  are statist and not political organisations), and whose real
  heterogeneous places are – at the very least – consensus-based
  (opinion) and the factory as a place of time, although the mode
  claims to possess only a single 'objective' place: the State;
- the Stalinist mode, which imposes the Party-State as a
  reference point for all subjectivity, all of whose heterogeneous
  places are places of the Party-State (hence its terrorist character) and whose sequence runs from the beginning of the
  1930s to the arrival of Gorbachev in power.

When it comes to the word 'worker', a long analysis establishes
that the category is the factory as a specified place. This analysis
is supported by numerous and varied inquests, led personally by
Lazarus in factories throughout the world (the inquest 'consists
in the placing of people and what they think in relation; this
placing in relation constitutes a face to face meeting'[25]). We can
distinguish (just as we distinguished different historical modes of
politics) the following places of the factory:

- the factory as a political place (a Shanghai factory of machine-
  tools during the Cultural Revolution, or a Gdansk naval
  dockyard at the time of Solidarity in Poland);

- the factory as a place of time (the parliamentary prescription regarding the factory);
- the factory as a place of the State (the prescription of the Stalinist mode);
- the factory as a place of money (in Canton at the time of Deng Xiaoping).

This category of 'factory' authorises the capture of the intellectuality of an unnameable name *which is not 'worker' as such, but the worker/factory pairing.* In the case of the factory as a place of the State, time or money (three specifications of place), the factory is always a subjective category, it is prescribed. But the term 'worker', the other component of the pairing, is objectified, either as a class collective (the factory as a place of the Socialist State), or again through evacuation [*l'absentement*] pure and simple (this is the case of the factory as a place of time, where there are no longer workers, only 'employees'). It is only when the factory is prescribed as a political place that the term 'worker' exists subjectively, in the form of the prescriptive statement: 'in the factory, there is the worker'. The place of such a statement is what Lazarus names the 'figure of the worker' [*la figure ouvrière*]. We can therefore conclude that the unnameable name is the factory/worker pairing, its category is the factory, while the factory as a specified place and the figure of the worker are the places of the pairing.

These fundamental results reveal the prolific intellectual framework set up by Sylvain Lazarus. The most precious singularities for asserting the freedom of thought (i.e. its vocation to prescribe a possible) are accessible here both through the exterior unity of a category (such as 'historical mode of politics' or 'specification of the factory'), which in turn refers to a multiple of singularities; and through the 'material' determination of their

places, which are akin to the assured inscription of their prescriptive nature. When we have thus conceptualised, notably,
singularities in interiority (those which do not abandon subjectivity, those which hold firm to the prescription, in other words,
the historical modes of politics as revolutionary, classist,
Bolshevik or dialectical; or, again, the different occurrences of
the figure of the worker) one is persuaded of the existence of *a
free access of thought to the material sequences of its own freedom.*

e) Against Historicism

That these formulations break fundamentally with the still
dominant forms of intellectuality gives us pause for consideration.

Sylvain Lazarus is persuaded that *historicism*, in one form or
another, dominates contemporary thought. Even when it comes
to an author as structuralist as Lévi-Strauss, whose project of
evacuating history is explicit, Lazarus locates a persistent, fundamental kernel of historicism the selection of which defines a
totality: society. But 'the category of society founds historicism,
whether one calls it "totality", "world" or "historical world".
The ambition of the social sciences is … to analyse the Real as
a heterogeneous multiple. The "there is" that they postulate is
both unique and composite.'[26] The break with historicism can
only be achieved by pursuing the thinkability of prescriptive singularities; by positing the Real, not as a composite or complex
unity, but as a 'certain indistinct', and by restricting oneself to
homogeneous multiplicities. It is absolutely essential to evacuate
'objective' unities such as 'society' or 'complex whole', and to
adhere strictly to the discipline of categories (such as 'historical
mode of politics'), which only relate to subjective singularities
and places that deploy unnameable names.

Little by little, Lazarus shows us how historicism is the internal principle of an entire series of intellectual configurations that we might regard as being innocent, or quite remote from its contagion:

- dialectics – that of the social sciences rather than Hegelian negativity – which is given in operators of reversibility between the subjective and the objective, such as 'consciousness', 'representations', 'mentalities', etc.;
- scientism, to the extent that it presupposes the typically historicist pairing of subject and object;
- circulating categories, like that of 'social class', which cement heterogeneous multiplicities, since they circulate between objectivity (analysis of the social whole in terms of classes) and subjectivity (class consciousness);
- the theory/practice pairing, which permits the ascent from the objective to the subjective (theory), then the descent from the subjective to the objective (practice), thus allowing for the reversible identification of politics and history, of the subjective and the State;
- finally, time, which co-presents the material and the mental.

Lazarus ably demonstrates how the installation of thought within these composite configurations necessarily supports the State, since history is ultimately a 'relation of the State'. It follows that any contemporary freedom of thought presupposes, by virtue of the rupture with the most subtle forms of historicism, a distancing of the State, of which one of the paradigms is the clear separation between politics (as thought) and the State.

The force of this critique is felt in the lucid responses that Lazarus is capable of providing to all sorts of questions from which our modernity is woven:

- Why did Althusser, whose overt intention was to think politics after Stalinism, no sooner than having inaugurated this question (by identifying politics at a distance from the Party-State apparatus, and by defining Lenin as a thinker of politics), ultimately fail? Because, by maintaining the 'structured whole in dominance' as the 'there is' for thought, he left the subjective (which he implicitly isolated) in the clutches of historicism.

- Why did an entire 'generation' of May '68 militants, who had previously been thrown into an ultra-activist Maoist ideologism, evidently come round to parliamentarianism in the form prescribed by Mitterrand? Because these militants, stuck in historicism, separated politics from thought (remaining in the theory/practice schema) and therefore required a third term in order to bind together a totality. They were activists as long as movements supplied them with this third term, between May '68 and the (workers') movement of Lip and the (peasant) movement of Larzac.[27] Totalisation, then, took the form of 'supporting' the movement. Mitterrand's State quite evidently became the relay for movements and their principle of totalisation. 'The passage from the problematic of the party to that of the movement, then the passage from that of the movement to that of parliamentary consensus, and from that of the parliamentary State to that of the State pure and simple, supports a single system: that of the split between the practical space of politics (henceforth called the "social") and the space of its intellectuality ...'.[28]

- Why was Foucault (whom Lazarus salutes as the 'first theoretician of singularities'[29]), after having isolated irreducible configurations with his category of *épistémè*, unable to achieve a true thought of interiority? Because after having posited that the operator for the identification of singularities was the relation of words to things, he did not localise this operator, and left unclear the *whereabouts* of the enunciated multiplicity of *épistémai*. The result of this omission is that the words/things relation remains external. Foucault's singularities (analysis of discursive formations, positivities and the corresponding knowledge) remain composite, lacking an identification of the prescriptive or subjective kernel that lies at their heart. Foucault did not *think his own thought*. But his immense merit was to have bequeathed us the question of how it might be done, since his teaching persuades us that 'declaring the existence of singularities does not resolve the problem of the thought which permits their investigation'.[30]

From these few brief examples we can already see the power of Lazarus' operators: they permit rigorous inquests into the avatars of modernity.

f) On the Name 'Politics'

Bearing in mind that 'politics' is one of the principal names whose thinkability Lazarus sets out, let us summarise his results.

The Anthropology of the Name is not politics, or rather it is not *a* politics. Lazarus does not cease to emphasise this point, all the more so since he is, as people are beginning to notice, an exemplary militant and political leader: 'Political questions have preoccupied me for a long time, and still do. However, the project of an anthropology of the name is not reducible to them.'[31] In *The Anthropology of the Name* politics is, precisely, only a name.

Nevertheless, *The Anthropology of the Name* prepares the context for seizing the intellectuality of a politics; it is the place for the identification of political singularities. Let us review the axial theses that structure this identification.

1. Since every politics is a singularity, there can be no definition of politics. Every definition relates politics to something other than itself (in fact, most often to the State), and desingularises it by historicising it.

2. Politics is a thought. This statement excludes all recourse to the theory/practice pairing. There is certainly a 'doing' of politics, but it is immediately the pure and simple experience of a thought, its localisation. Doing politics cannot be distinguished from thinking politics.

3. The problem is not the being of this thought, but its thinkability. Can politics be thought *as* thought? That is the question.

4. The category pertaining to this thinkability is that of the historical mode of politics. The mode is defined as the relation of a politics to its thought, which may itself be apprehended through categories internal to political subjectivity (virtue and corruption for Saint-Just, revolutionary consciousness as a condition for Lenin, etc.). The mode designates the sequential character and rarity of politics as thought. Politics is precarious, the mode begins and terminates, without this termination ever amounting to a measure of the mode, or there ever being cause to speak of failure:

> The problematic of failure does not permit factual verification; instead of treating the fact as a unit, it carves it out in its own way. The termination of a politics is not enough to identify it. On the contrary, it is essential to think the termination of all politics. Termination, then, is no longer a litmus test, but rather that which comes about at the end of the sequence and constitutes the idea of sequence.[32]

5. The mode is a category which refers to rare singularities, and which authorises their seizure in thought. This does not mean that the historicity of politics – its subjective efficacy, which is the Real of its name – is thereby conceptualised. For this would presume that a politics can be the real *object* of thought, or, what comes down to the same thing, that the name is nameable. Historicity is outside the scope of the investigation, the name is not presented directly within it. But its intellectuality is conceptualised. The political singularities make up the multiplicity proper to the category of historical mode of politics.

6. A politics, as an unnameable name, is not reducible to the mode, which is the category of the name. 'The thought of the mode from the point of existence is politics and its field. The thought of the mode from the point of its lapsing is to be found in terms of a name and a place of the name.'[33] One can therefore distinguish the exercise of thought in the form of the mode 'taking-place' and in the form of the mode 'having-taken-place', i.e. the closed or bygone mode. In the second case, that of a bygone mode, we enter into the thinking of politics from the point of view of categories which uphold the relation of a politics to its thought. In the case of a mode taking-place (the investigation of the contemporary), one enters into politics as thought through *one* of the places of the name and through the basic prescription that determines it, within subjectivity, as a place. A contemporary politics is always *politics-there* [*politique-là*]. Its 'doing', which is the same thing as its thought, prescribes the place. For example, in the case of the worker/factory pairing, it declares that the factory is a political place that produces singular statements which bring forth the other place – in other words the figure of the worker – statements that are upheld by the maxim: 'in the factory, there is the worker'. But although the points of

entry differ (in the taking-place we have politics and its field, thinkable by way of places; while in the having-taken-place, we have a 'descent' towards the places by way of the identification of the mode as the relation of a politics to its thought) *the intellectuality in question remains homogeneous*, and is always organised, along distinct paths, by the following ensemble: mode/name/ places of the name. Let us quote from the key synthetic conclusion, which *guarantees that the distinction between taking-place and having-taken-place allows us to avoid passing through either history or time.* Politics taking-place is a subjectification, while thinking through the determination of the mode of a politics having-taken-place is a subjectification of subjectification, which is established in interiority and within the space of the same categories:

> The configuration of the name and the places of the name is the one in which, when politics terminates, the name terminates on the grounds that so does the mode. Of course, the fact that the mode possessed places [*le mode ait eu des lieux*] is not thereby abolished. Of course, the termination carries off the name while it remains the case that the place possessed places [*le lieu ait eu des lieux*]. But the fact that the name possessed places anchors the termination in subjectification, or in a singular intellectuality .... Beyond termination, the mode is thinkable in a subjectification of subjectification. And this movement is what ensures that subjectification is not consubstantial to the existence of the mode, but rather coextensive to its thought and that which renders its thought thinkable. If thought is thinkable, this thinkability operates beyond the mode's termination.[34]

Such is the principal gain of the disjunction between politics and history, and of the abolition of the category of time: the seizure in thought of a politics remains a homogeneous operation, whether it involves an 'ongoing' politics or a bygone politics, even if the accompanying protocols are distinct from one another. In any case, politics is only thinkable through itself.

7. Every contemporary politics has the factory as its place. In the parliamentary mode of politics, the factory is prescribed as a place of time, and the figure of the worker is evacuated (this is the underlying meaning of the qualification by the Mitterrand–Mauroy government, in 1984, of the strikes at Renault-Flins and Talbot-Poissy,[35] as strikes led by 'immigrants' or 'Shiites'). According to the hypothesis of an interior politics, such as the one promoted by the Organisation Politique, the factory is prescribed as a political place, and the figure of the worker is localised therein through singular statements.

Evidently these theses do not constitute any politics by themselves, rather they maintain the gap between the anthropology of the name and politics. However, they do affirm the thinkability of instances of politics and constitute the intellectual field through which their singularity may be grasped.

g) And Philosophy?

The question I wish to address to this foundational work is, obviously, that of a philosopher. The whole point, in my view, is knowing whether *The Anthropology of the Name* falls under an anti-philosophical framework (like Lacan's Analysis, for example, or the thematic of the 'mystical element' in Wittgenstein's *Tractatus*). 'Anti-philosophy' certainly does not offend me, since it represents the major determination, in my view, of works of the calibre of Pascal, Rousseau, Kierkegaard, Nietzsche, Wittgenstein or Lacan. Sylvain Lazarus unequivocally defends himself against falling under this determination. On the one hand, he insists on the fact that the anthropology of the name is not in the least a philosophy, even though he considers anti-philosophers philosophers of a particular type. On the other hand, he declares himself a 'friend of philosophy', and takes great care, for example, not to confuse what he declares as being terminated or lapsed (i.e. the historicist dialectic in the social sciences, which works on composite and heterogeneous multiplicities) with Hegelian negativity, which seems to him, on the contrary, to rely on a thought of the homogeneous. This is, moreover, equally true of the Platonic theory of ideas, or of my own axiomatic theory of the pure multiple.

However, the question is difficult.

Philosophy and the anthropology of the name certainly share the statement which Lazarus calls Statement 1, which declares: 'people think'. Recall that Spinoza maintains as an axiom the phrase '*homo cogitat*', and formulates it as such. Man thinks. But Lazarus considers as absolutely specific to the anthropology of the name Statement 2: 'thought is a relation of the Real'. Must we not then conclude from this (which formally marks the start of all proceedings brought against philosophy by any anti-philosopher worthy of the name) that philosophy as thought, or that which is thought in philosophy as thought, does not touch upon any Real whatsoever? Thus, for Wittgenstein, philosophical statements are meaningless inasmuch as they claim to restrict the form of the proposition to a non-pliant, trans-mundane Real, which is indicated only by way of silence. Likewise, Lacan considers that philosophy wants nothing to do with the Real of *jouissance*.

Admittedly, Lazarus says nothing of the kind. The protocol of separation between philosophy, history and the anthropology of the name contains no negative criteria:

There exists a multiplicity of rationalisms. All possess a Statement 2, or rather each rationalism constructs its own category of the Real, which is internal to its two statements, taken in their unity and in their succession. I will say, for example, that philosophy is a thought-relation-of-thought [*une pensée-rapport-de-la-pensée*]; history is a thought-relation-of-the-State. As for the anthropology of the name, I try to establish it as a thought-relation-of-the-Real.[36]

Who could fail to recognise that 'Real' occurs twice in this schema? Philosophy, it would seem, constructs its Real as 'thought', while history constructs it in the name of the State. Only the anthropology of the name, if I can put it like this, constructs its Real ... as Real. It is only in the anthropology of the name that the construction of the Real has 'Real' as its simple name. This clearly indicates that for Lazarus – however much of a 'friend' of philosophy he may be – philosophical rationalism hardly enjoys the same 'proximity' to the Real (characterised as indistinction rather than as object) as the new, anti-dialectical rationalism that he calls 'anthropology of the name'. I even suspect that history, which is after all Lazarus' key interlocutor – since his whole project is to de-historicise the thought of singularities – maintains for him, within the space of the State, tighter and more disputable bonds with the anthropology of the name than philosophy can ever claim to have. Lazarus draws considerable support from Moses Finley, the great historian of antiquity, as well as from Marc Bloch, and even from the historiography of the French Revolution, despite his criticisms of it. The two contemporary 'philosophers' skilfully studied in his book are Althusser and Foucault. But as to the first, it must be said that what captivates Lazarus is Althusser's singular effort to make politics after Stalin thinkable, and certainly not the post-Bachelardian attempt to make 'science' the name for the multiple of thoughts. As for the second, who could fail to recognise that Foucault 'twisted' philosophy towards an archival history of epistemic singularities, that he was more of a historian than any of us, to the extent that nowadays his followers are much more active in the profession of the 'human sciences' than in 'pure' philosophy? Besides, everybody knows that Foucault's real philosophical referent was Nietzsche and that, despite the latter's silent latency in Foucault's published work, Foucault is the Prince of contemporary anti-philosophy.

Let us add that, for Lazarus, philosophy inevitably proceeds by way of concepts (this is why thinking philosophy can only be a relation of thought). But we know that, for the anthropology of the name, the concept (as distinct from the category) is generally exportable, falls under the heading of heterogeneous multiplicity and, finally, always lacks singularity.

Formulated in my own terms (which are inevitably those of philosophy), the question then becomes the following. For me, a singularity is a truth, or more precisely a truth procedure. For example, I recognise clearly how the historical modes of politics effectively identified by Lazarus overlap with what I name political truth procedures. Given the fact we have been political cohorts for twenty years, it is not surprising that such overlaps are apparent! My thought on this point is sustained, purely and simply, by that of Lazarus. For my part, I recognise other singularities that Lazarus, in *The Anthropology of the Name*, does not account for: artistic configurations, scientific theories and amorous episodes ('configuration', 'theory', 'episode' are concepts – categories? – which in each instance relate to multiple singularities). Philosophy is conditioned by these singularities in that its intention is always 'to seize' (to indicate), through conceptual operations which are themselves invented, or singular, the existence and the compossibility of truths, contemporary truths, *taking-place*. Thereby philosophy evaluates and thinks whatever its time is capable of by way of truths (of singularities).

So what role does the anthropology of the name have within this configuration? For the anthropology of the name, at least with regard to political singularities, aspires to a good deal more than simply being conditioned by them. It claims *to think singularity itself*, not through concepts, but through subjectifying the subjectification at work within this singularity. Inasmuch as it then becomes the subjective efficacy of a thought of thought, how could the anthropology of the name not enter into rivalry with philosophy, whose own constitutive statement is – as previously noted – that thought is a relation of thought? We must no doubt admit that if the anthropology of the name is possible, *it dominates* [*surplombe*] *philosophy*, not at all by subsuming the latter (which is what Lacan claims to do, for example), but by attaining, through non-philosophical (non-conceptual) means, a superior intellectual mastery of philosophy's truth conditions.

Am I going to conclude, solely motivated by the vain desire to protect philosophy, that the anthropology of the name is impossible? Certainly not, since it exists in its categories, its inquests, and its results. Rather, I prefer *to situate the anthropology of the name within the conditions of philosophy*, through an uncoupling which is itself philosophically foundational. I have already had occasion to practise this strategy in the case of psychoanalysis, as overhauled by Lacan. Lacan's undertaking permits a much closer study of one of the conditions of philosophical truth: namely, that of love. Today, placing philosophy under condition of love as truth is unthinkable (or it evades the demand of taking-place, of the contemporary) if one neglects the radical undertaking through which Lacan organises in thought the quasi-ontological encounter [*face-à-face*] of love and desire. It is clear that Lazarus' thought does for politics what Lacan has done for love: he organises its disjunctive encounter with history. The result of this is that to place philosophy under condition of politics as truth is today unthinkable, or non-modern, if one neglects Lazarus' undertaking.

The fact that Lazarus displays nothing but contempt for the category of truth (about which he constantly declares, in the tradition of all anti-philosophers, that it is entirely useless for his purposes) does not bother me at all. For *no truth procedure has 'truth' as an internal category*. 'Truth' is a philosophical word (the same goes for 'event', a word which neither Lazarus nor Lacan makes the least categorical use of). Putting philosophy under condition of politics 'taking-place' (or politics as an infinite unfinished procedure) will pass through the anthropology of the name, inasmuch as one will entrust the latter to identify – by way of modes, names and places of the name – singularity at work. One will then seize this singularity *in toto* as truth (and as the manifestation of a singular eventality) within the space of philosophy, wherein singularity thereby affects and compels major conceptual readjustments.

Let us be even more provocative (but the provocation is only the true recognition of the fact that rationalisms are effectively multiple). For Lazarus it is essential that a politics, conceptualised on the basis of its own practice, is never defined, and that the word 'politics' remains unnameable. Philosophy, by complete contrast, never ceases to define politics, because this comprises the immanent mode through which it places itself under condition of real politics. Today, to place philosophy under condition of the anthropology of the name is to achieve what this anthropology absolutely prohibits: an entirely renewed definition of politics. Of course, we will concede that this definition is completely philosophical and consequently has no interest outside itself. Specifically: no political interest. Didn't Althusser say that the effects of philosophy are immanent, that they are always *philosophical* even though, in order to remain philosophical, these effects are no less real?

There always comes a time, the time of places and effects, when a thought 'relation of thought' intersects with a thought 'relation of the Real' without merging with it. In the same way, Lazarus' thought and mine first crossed paths as long ago as 1970, and have not ceased to intersect ever since with fraternal effects.

It is in any case under the jurisdiction of these points of recurrent intersection, themselves cemented by real political processes, that I have learnt how to relate philosophically to politics only under condition of politics. Accordingly, what is at stake here is what I name metapolitics, or what, in philosophy, carries a trace of a political condition which is neither an object nor what requires production in thought, but only a contemporaneity that produces philosophical *effects*.

But wasn't Althusser's strange undertaking (to which Lazarus does not cease to pay homage) already, and from an early stage, the project of a metapolitical, or philosophical, relation to politics as real thought? For a long time I opposed head on the self-imposed inertia I detected in the relationship of this undertaking with the French Communist Party. In hindsight, I am better placed to see what we others, those philosophical enemies of political philosophy, owe Althusser.

Notes

1 A version of this text was originally published as 'Penser la singularité: Les noms innommables' in *Critique* 595 (December 1996), pp. 1074–95.

2 Sylvain Lazarus, *L'Anthropologie du nom*, Paris: Seuil, 1996.

3 Ibid., p. 52.

4 Ibid., p. 81.

5 Ibid., p. 80.

6 Ibid., p. 119.

7 Ibid., p. 119.

8 Ibid., p. 160.

9 Ibid., p. 17.

10 Ibid., p. 15.

11 Ibid., p. 66.

12 Ibid., p. 16.

13 Ibid., 138.

14 Ibid., p. 192.

15 Ibid., p. 157.

16 Ibid., p. 158.

17 Ibid.

18 Ibid., p. 192.

19 Ibid., p. 152.

20 Ibid.

21 Ibid.

22 Ibid., p. 89.

23 Ibid., p. 162.

24 Mao Tse-tung, 'Why Can China's Red Political Power Exist' in *Selected Works*, Vol I, London: Lawrence and Wishart, 1954, pp. 63–70.

25 Lazarus, *L'Anthropologie du nom*, p. 72.

26 Ibid., p. 193.

27 Lip was a watch factory in Besançon, France, which defied closure in 1973 when the workforce occupied the factory and began running it themselves. Larzac is a region of southern France that attracted a broad coalition of many thousands of protesters, throughout the 1970s, against the requisition of peasant land for a military training camp. *Trans*.

28 Ibid., p. 32.

29 Ibid., p. 104.

30 Ibid., p. 106.

31 Ibid., p. 15.

32 Ibid., p. 156.

33 Ibid., p. 51.

34 Ibid.

35 See *Peut-on penser la politique?* Paris: Seuil, 1985, pp. 69–76. *Trans.*

36 Lazarus, *L'Anthropologie du nom*, p. 17.

3

Althusser:
Subjectivity without a Subject

Leaving aside the countless obscene onlookers for whom Althusser has become a mere pathological case bequeathed to the collectors of unusual psyches, it seems to me that two ideas dominate research into his theoretical work, research that has been carried out with an international zeal which – this is a good sign – has yet to falter.

The first is to place Althusser in relation to Marxism.

The second is to try to find in his work a theory of the subject.

On the first point I believe, to put it quite bluntly, that *Marxism doesn't exist*. As I have already mentioned, Sylvain Lazarus has established that between Marx and Lenin there is rupture and foundation rather than continuity and development. Equally, there is rupture between Stalin and Lenin, and between Mao and Stalin. Althusser represents yet another attempt at rupture. And what complicates the picture even more is that all of these ruptures are themselves different in kind. All of which makes 'Marxism' the (void) name of an absolutely inconsistent set, once it is referred back, as it must be, to the history of political singularities.

Moreover, it is important to note that the project of a 'Marxist philosophy', at one time heralded by Althusser, was one he abandoned. Althusser explains perfectly, in *Lenin and Philosophy*,[1] that Marx and Lenin did not inaugurate a new philosophy, but a new *practice* of philosophy, which is a different thing entirely and relates to politics.

This means that it is impossible to penetrate Althusser's work if one considers it as a 'case' of Marxism, or as the (incomplete) testimony of a Marxist philosophy. In order to penetrate Althusser's work we must consider the singularity of his undertaking and his wholly particular aims.

The preliminary question is therefore the following: *how* – from what cognitive place – is one able to grasp Althusser's singularity? How is this to be done without resorting to the *a priori*, and namely to the *a priori* of Marxism?

On the second point, my verdict is stark: there is no theory of the subject in Althusser, nor could there ever be one.

For Althusser, all theory proceeds by way of concepts. But 'subject' is not a concept. This theme is developed with the utmost clarity in 'Marx's Relation to Hegel'. For example: 'the concept "process" is scientific, the notion "subject" is ideological'.[2] 'Subject' is not the name of a concept, but that of a notion, that is, the mark of an inexistence. There is no subject, since there are only processes.

The very frequent attempt to supplement Althusser with Lacan on this question, which seeks support in some of Althusser's passages on psychoanalysis, is in my view unworkable. In Lacan there is a theoretical concept of the subject, which even has an ontological status. For the being of the subject in Lacan is the coupling of the void and the 'objet petit a'. There is no such thing in Althusser, for whom the object exists even less than the subject. Althusser writes: 'object = a mirror reflection of *subject*.[3] The object is therefore the image of an inexistence. The process without a subject functions just as effectively as the process without an object.

The second preliminary question, under these conditions, is the following: if there is no subject, if there are only processes without a subject, how are we to distinguish politics from the science of processes without a subject, that is to say, from the science of history, in the form of historical materialism? How do we distinguish politics from (the) science (of historical materialism) without, quite obviously, reducing it to ideology?

Now, that politics is neither science nor ideology is a conviction constantly asserted by Althusser. In 1965, he distinguished political practice from ideological practice and scientific practice. In 1968, he explained that every process is 'in relations',[4] relations that might be the relations of production, but also other relations: political, or ideological, here once again distinguished from one another.

Better still: Althusser posits that only the 'militants of the revolutionary class struggle' really grasp the thought of the process in relations. Therefore, genuine thought of process is possessed by those engaged in political practice.

Finally, there are three points whose unity must be grasped thoroughly. First, politics is distinct from both science and ideology. Second, the notion of subject is unable to ground these distinctions. Third, it is through politics that the notion of 'process in relations' is thinkable.

Let us maintain, then, that every 'thinking' [*pensant*] relation to Althusser must begin by dealing with two questions. First, there is the question of the singularity of his undertaking, to be conceived quite differently than as a case of the void name 'Marxism'. And second, within this singularity, is the question of politics as a process without a subject, bearing in mind that the political process alone is capable, in its militant dimension, of granting access to the *thought* of what, in general, a process without a subject is.

Let us provide some directions on these two preconditions.

The place from which Althusser is speaking is philosophy. Like all philosophy, Althusser's aims to provide a definition of philosophy itself. And everyone knows that Althusser provided (at least) *two* definitions of philosophy.

The first is 'theory of theoretical practice'.[5] This definition remains within the scope of dialectical materialism as a formal synthesis of the processes of thought.

The second is 'representation of the class struggle with the sciences' [*représentation de la lutte des classes auprès des sciences*].[6] Or: representation, vis-à-vis the sciences, of politics. This definition means that the fundamental condition for philosophical activity is its dependence on politics, on political clarification. Althusser's project thereby becomes the attempt to think the characteristics of politics after Stalin *under the aegis of a philosophical rupture*.

Why is this project tenable? Precisely because what happens in philosophy is organically bound to the political condition of philosophy. Thus, one can treat philosophy, from within itself, as a kind of recording apparatus of its own political condition. In particular, a new philosophical possibility might allow itself to be deciphered – albeit at the expense of a complex 'torsion' – as the intra-philosophical index of a real movement of the political condition. For Althusser, the hope was that a new philosophical activity would come to bear witness to what was *in the process of becoming thinkable* in politics after Stalin.

In order to grasp every nuance of this project, it is crucial not to confuse it with that of a political philosophy, and it is on this point that the rupture brought about by Althusser anticipates the guiding questions of our own metapolitics. That

philosophy could be the place where politics after Stalin is
thought is utterly rejected by Althusser. Indeed, only political
militants think political novelty effectively. What philosophy *is*
able to do is to record, in the unfolding of previously unseen
philosophical possibilities, the sign of a renewed 'thinkability'
(as Lazarus says) of politics *conceived on the basis of its own exercise.*
Althusser knew very well that whoever claims that philosophy
directly thinks politics – consequently renamed 'the political' –
simply submits philosophy to the objectivity of the State. If
philosophy is able to record what happens in politics, it is precisely because philosophy is not a theory of politics, but a *sui
generis* activity of thought which finds itself conditioned by the
events of real politics (events of the class struggle, in Althusser's
vocabulary). And it is through being made to fulfil its seismo-
graphic function vis-à-vis the real movements of thinkable
politics that Althusser will construct a very special arrangement
that philosophy will be required to assume:

- Philosophy is not a theory, but a separating activity, a thinking
  of the distinctions in thought. Therefore it can by no means
  theorise politics. But it can draw new lines of partition, think
  new distinctions, which verify the 'shifting' of the political
  condition.
- Philosophy has no object. In particular, the 'political' object
  does not exist for it. Philosophy is an act whose effects are
  strictly immanent. It is the discovery of new possibles *in actu*
  which bends philosophy towards its political condition.
- Philosophy is guarded from the danger of confusing history
  and politics (therefore science and politics) on account of itself
  lacking history. Philosophy authorises a non-historicist per-
  ception of political events.

On all of these points, Althusser's philosophical singularity is extremely strong, and is far from having produced its full range of effects. Every truly contemporary philosophy must set out from the singular theses according to which Althusser identifies philosophy.

Seeing that Althusser's project is to identify politics through its immanent effects within philosophical activity, the first phase of this project is essentially in the order of *separation*. The task here is to demonstrate how politics distinguishes itself from both ideology and science, and to do so through acts (therefore theses) of a philosophical character.

For Althusser, science is characterised by the conceptual construction of its objects. If 'object', taken in the general sense, is an ideological notion (correlated with the inexistence of the subject), in another sense 'object' (this time correlated, in the absence of any subject, with 'objectivity') designates the very kernel of scientific practice. Science is a process without a subject but with objects, and objectivity is its specific norm. To distinguish politics from science is first to recognise that politics, just like philosophy, has no object and does not submit to the norm of objectivity. Althusser designates the non-objective norm of politics with the expressions 'partisanship', '(class) position' or '(revolutionary) militant activity'.

(Bourgeois) ideology is characterised by the notion of subject, whose matrix is legal and which subjects the individual to the ideological State apparatuses: this is the theme of 'subjective interpellation' [*interpellation en sujet*]. It is crucial to note that ideology, whose materiality is provided by the apparatuses, *is a statist notion*, and not a political notion. The subject, in Althusser's sense, is a function of the State. Thus, there will be no political subject, because revolutionary politics cannot be a function of the State.

The whole problem, then, is the following: how do we designate the singular space of politics if it is subtracted from the object and objectivity (politics is not science) as well as from the subject (politics is not ideology, is not a function of the State)? In practice, and in a patently incomplete manner, Althusser approached this question in the following two ways.

1. 'Class' and 'class struggle' are the signifiers that constantly 'harness' the fleeting identity of politics. They are the names of politics. The word 'struggle' indicates that there is no political object (a struggle is not an object), and the word 'class' indicates that there is no subject either (Althusser opposed any idea of the proletariat-subject in the field of history). This nominal identification is strictly provisional, even doubtful, for a reason persuasively advanced by Lazarus: the word 'class' circulates, inducing ambivalence between the science of history (of which it is a concept relating to the construction of an object) and politics.

2. With expressions like 'partisanship', 'choice', 'decision' or 'revolutionary militant', Althusser *indicates* that what is involved in politics is well and truly of the subjective order.

Let us say that the point to which Althusser leads us, without being able to say that he realised it himself, is the following: is it possible to think *subjectivity without a subject*? What's more, is it possible to think subjectivity without a subject whose figure is no longer the (scientific) object? It is towards this enigma of subjectivity without a subject as the intra-philosophical mark of politics that the whole of what might be termed Althusser's *topographical* framework [*l'appareillage topique*] is directed.

According to the doctrine of the 'It's all there already', the topographical structuring brings to light three essential points:

1. A materialist determination by the economy, which provides a principle of massive stability. In fact, the economy is the figure of objectivity, the place of the object, and therefore the place of science.

2. Imaginary syntheses, borne by individuals, who are nominal inexistents. This is the place of the subject, the place of ideology. It is also that of the State in its operational range, in its 'take' over singular bodies, in the functional (and not principally objective) existence of its apparatuses.

3. Evental overdeterminations, catastrophes, revolutions, novelties, becoming-principal of the non-principal contradiction. Here lies the real stuff of partisanship, the militant's opportunity, the moment of choice. Overdetermination puts the possible on the agenda, whereas the economic place (objectivity) is that of well-ordered stability, and the statist place (ideological subjectivity) makes individuals 'function'. Overdetermination is in truth the political place. And it must indeed be said that overdetermination belongs to the subjective realm (choice, partisanship, militancy), even though it knows no subject-effect (such effects are statist), nor does it verify, or construct, any object (such objects only exist in the field of science).

How should 'subjectivity' without a subject or object be understood here? It is a process of homogeneous thought in the material form of militancy, one not determined through (scientific) objectivity, nor captive to the (ideological) subject-effect. At the place of overdetermination [*au lieu de la surdétermination*], this process balances over into the possible, and does so in accordance with a partisanship, a prescription, that nothing guarantees, neither in the objective order of the economy nor in the statist order of the subject, but which nonetheless is capable of tracing a real trajectory in the situation.

Althusser did not think this place, as Lazarus attempts to do today, through a foundational approach that abandons the philosophical detour. But he did seek a speculative topography which, broadening, or as he said 'fulfilling', the vision of Marx and Engels, makes thinking this vision possible. Not directly (for in reality Althusser wasn't politically active), but within the realm inferred from philosophical registration.

For the time it was quite some project, and it still focuses our intellectual tasks to this day. This admirable effort, as yet unnamed (to think subjectivity without a subject), is enough to make Louis Althusser worthy of our most rigorous respect. For it was he who provided access to these difficult efforts which attempt, outside all political philosophy, to bring new, politically conditioned, philosophical effects to life. It was also following his lead that we became obliged to reject the humanist vision of the bond, or the being-together, which binds an abstract and ultimately enslaved vision of politics to the theological ethics of rights.

It is for this reason that I shall dedicate the following two metapolitical exercises to Althusser, devoted to the notions of 'political bond' and democracy respectively.

Notes

1 Louis Althusser, *Lenin and Philosophy and Other Essays*, trans. Ben Brewster. London: NLB, 1971.

2 Louis Althusser, 'Marx's Relation to Hegel', in *Politics and History.*
   Montesquieu, Rousseau, Hegel, Marx, trans. Ben Brewster. London:
   NLB, 1972, p. 185.
3 Ibid.
4 Ibid., p. 186.
5 Louis Althusser, *For Marx*, trans. Ben Brewster. London: NLB,
   1969; Althusser and Étienne Balibar, *Reading Capital*, trans. Ben
   Brewster. London: NLB, 1970.
6 Althusser, 'Lenin and Philosophy', in *Lenin and Philosophy and Other*
   Essays, p. 65.

Politics Unbound

In this chapter I shall place philosophy under condition of politics. Not exactly the most contemporary of politics, but the one that can be called the 'first cycle' of modern emancipatory politics, the revolutionary and proletarian cycle, the one to which the names of Marx, Lenin and Mao remain attached. Bear in mind that, as we have already mentioned, each one of these names designates a singular sequence of politics, a historical mode of its rare existence, even if philosophy occasionally seeks to bridge this essential discontinuity for its own ends.

The two essential parameters for these political sequences, and particularly for the one that bears the name of Mao, are the masses and the party. The latter terms, moreover, are most often targeted by the contemporary hostility towards revolutionary politics, reduced by a few propagandists posing as historians to the single moral category of 'crime'.

In the case of the 'masses', the objection is either that they function as nothing but a pure signifier, intended to make the intellectual submit to the injunction to 'join with the masses', or that, as something real and uncontrollable, they function as a blind cluster exposed through the imaginary cement of its coalescence to idolatry, cruelty, folly and, finally, to the abjection of dissolution and renunciation.

In the case of the (Leninist) 'party', the objection is that it's the representative fiction that gives rise to disciplinary asceticism, the end of critical examination, the reign of petty bureaucrats and, finally, a fusion with the State whence proceeds a bureaucratic machinery which is both brutish and paralytic.

In both cases, it is the fact that these terms are presented under the aegis of the one, of the primordial bond – of the one within the bond – which makes them into terms of enslavement or decomposition. It is through lack of adequate symbolism and reference to what is right, to the rule, and hence to the dispersal of cases, that masses and party oscillate between the barbarism of the pure Real and the grandiose deception of the Imaginary. Or rather: the masses/party pairing conjoins both, ultimately leading us to idolise the crime as the Real consecrated by the image, or a simulacrum that declares itself the embodiment of meaning.

Granted. But if 'masses' and 'party' can designate, and have widely designated, real phenomena of this order, was it really on account of the political signification of these terms? It has often been remarked that what characterised Soviet society was the death of politics rather than politics being 'placed in command'. And the assessment of the Cultural Revolution in China concerns the question of knowing whether the complex of ideology and the economy, which was, after all, crystallised in the slogan 'red and expert', may not have widely eclipsed the strictly political rationale of these processes.

What such gigantic historical phenomena testify to may well be, not the triumphal and sinister power of the political articulation masses/party, but rather the extreme political weakness of an entire epoch, the Marxist-Leninist or Stalinist epoch, which with respect to what is required in order to unearth the being of politics, would appear to have been equivalent to the strictly metaphysical epoch of this lost ontology; the epoch resulting from the Marxist event, or the epoch wherein politics is conducted only as the forgetting of politics. Furthermore, the conceptual form of this forgetting would appear to be due to the fact that its key signifiers, 'masses' and 'party', reorganised through the figure of the bond, would have been depoliticised and rearticulated, not in terms of being, but through the submission of politics to its 'supreme being', its god, or the State.

Rather than purely and simply renouncing politics, including its supreme signifiers 'masses' and 'party', about which Mao said that all political consciousness lay in trusting them, it is shrewder and more progressive to attempt to deconstruct the statist charge with which they came to be invested, and to rediscover their original, strictly political signification.

More precisely, we must ask the question that, without a doubt, constitutes the great enigma of the century: why does the subsumption of politics, either through the form of the immediate bond (the masses), or the mediate bond (the party), ultimately give rise to bureaucratic submission and the cult of the State? Why do the most heroic popular uprisings, the most persistent wars of liberation, the most indisputable mobilisations in the name of justice and liberty end – even if this is something beyond the confines of their own internalised sequence – in opaque statist constructions wherein none of the factors that gave meaning and possibility to their historical genesis is decipherable? Those who imagine themselves being able to settle these questions with a few evasive replies on totalitarian ideology would be more convincing if only it were not so apparent that they had simply abandoned the ideas of justice and the emancipation of humanity and had joined the eternal cohort of conservatives bent on preserving the 'lesser evil'. These questions can only be clarified by affirming the hypothesis according to which emancipatory politics, however rare and sequential it may be, does indeed exist, lest we start to resemble a doctor who, unable to comprehend the workings of cancer, ultimately declares it better to stick to herbal teas, crystal therapy or prayers to the Virgin Mary. The truth is that as soon as it becomes a question of politics, our society is full of these types of obscurantists: they seem to have understood once and for all that to strive for nothing beyond what is has always been the surest way not to fail. And, indeed, for the patient who prays to the Virgin and gets better, all well and good; but if the patient dies it is because She willed it. Similarly, if I implore our State to be good towards workers and illegal immigrants [*sans-papiers*], either it does something, and it's wonderful, or it does nothing, in which case this is put down to the merciless law of reality in crisis-ridden times. Either way, I have done my duty.

Let us do ours, which is a little more complicated.

The way in which the theme of the bond enters into the consideration of the 'masses' is through the substitution of this term for another, quite different one, which is the 'mass movement'. The imaginary attributes of gathering, cruelty, folly, and so on, are ascribed to the masses insofar as they rise up, join forces, riot. It is solely from the movement of the masses that we infer that mass politics exists through the totalisable figure of the bond. Sartre provided an exemplary glorification of this figure of identificatory transparency with the name 'group-in-fusion'. But was Sartre, who claimed to found a logic of history, a theoretician of politics? Is a mass movement, in itself, a political moment? That 'mass movement' is one of the terms from the field of politics – as is the State, moreover – is indisputable. Every popular movement of any scope sets politics new and immediate tasks, as do decisions taken by the State. However, it by no means follows that the mass movement is in itself a political phenomenon, any more than it follows that the State is, in itself, political – and, in fact, it is not. The mass movement as such is a historical phenomenon, and *may* be an event for politics. But what is *for* politics is not yet politically qualifiable.

Let us therefore declare that even though 'masses' was indeed a political concept, it was never the mass movement that was directly involved. I shall say instead, in my metapolitical language, which records the political condition in conformity with the parameters of ontology, that the mass movement is a specific mode of the 'inconsistent consistency' of the multiple insofar as it is historically presented. It is a multiple on the edge of the void, a historical event site. The mass movement, being presented but not re-presentable (by the State), verifies that the void roams around in presentation, which interests politics only to the extent that it is interested in the void itself as a point of being of historical presentation. And politics is interested in this point of being only because its task consists in remaining faithful to a dysfunction of the 'counting as one', to a flaw in the structure, quite simply because it is there that it uncovers the wherewithal for prescribing new possibles. One cannot infer from this indirect interest that a multiplicity on the edge of the void is, in itself, political.

Even if it is obvious that the bond is constitutive of the mass movement, it does not follow that it is constitutive of politics. On the contrary, more often than not it is only by breaking the presumed bond through which the mass movement operates that politics ensures the long-term durability of the event. Even at the heart of the mass movement, political activity is an unbinding, and is experienced as such by the movement. This is also why in the final analysis, and in terms of the sequence we are talking about here, which once again includes May '68 and its aftermath, 'mass leaders' were not the same type of men as political leaders.

In what sense, then, is, or was, 'masses' a signifier of politics? To say that politics is 'of the masses' simply means that, unlike bourgeois administration, it sets itself the task of involving people's consciousness in its process, and of taking directly into consideration the real lives of the dominated. In other words, 'masses', understood politically, far from gathering homogeneous crowds under some imaginary emblem, designates the infinity of intellectual and practical singularities demanded by and executed within every politics of justice. If bourgeois administration is not 'of the masses' it is not because it fails to gather people together – on the contrary, it is perfectly proficient at doing so when it needs to. It is because such administration, effective solely on the basis of power and the State, never concerns infinite singularity, either in its process or its aims. Administration, which is homogeneous to the state of the situation, deals with the parts, the subsets. By complete contrast, politics deals with the masses, because politics is unbound from the State, and diagonal to its parts. 'Masses' is therefore a signifier of extreme particularity, of the non-bond, and this is what makes it a political signifier.

Politics will always strive to deconstruct the bond, including the one within the mass movement, the better to detect those ramified divisions that attest to the mass-being of strictly political consciousness. Politics is a mass procedure because all singularity calls for it, and because its axiom, both straightforward and difficult, is that people think. Administration cares nothing for this, because it considers only the interests of parts. We can therefore say that politics is of the masses, not because it takes into account the 'interests of the greatest number', but because it is founded on the verifiable supposition that no one is enslaved, whether in thought or in deed, by the bond that results from those interests that are a mere function of one's place.

Mass politics therefore grapples with the bound consistency of parts in order to undo its illusory hold and to deploy every affirmative singularity presented by the multiple on the edge of the void. It is through such singularities, whose latent void is articulated by the event, that politics constructs the new law that subtracts itself from the State's authority.

The relation between 'organisation' and 'bond', or how the organised character of politics should be conceived, cannot be dealt with here. My only aim is to pull the Leninist theme of the party free from its Marxist-Leninist image and its Stalinist myth.

It is crucial to emphasise that for Marx or Lenin, who are both in agreement on this point, the real characteristic of the party is not its firmness, but rather its porosity to the event, its dispersive flexibility in the face of unforeseeable circumstances.

For the Marx of 1848, that which is named 'party' has no form of bond even in the institutional sense. The 'Communist Party', whose *Manifesto* Marx draws up, is immediately multiple since it comprises the most radical singularities from all the 'workers' parties'. The definition of the party refers purely to historical mobility, whose communist consciousness ensures both its international dimension (and hence its maximal 'multiple extension') and the direction of its global movement (and hence its unbinding from immediate interests). Thus, rather than referring to a dense, bound fraction of the working class – what Stalin will call a 'detachment' – the party refers to an unfixable omnipresence, whose proper function is less to represent class than to de-limit it by ensuring it is equal to everything that history presents as improbable and excessive in respect of the rigidity of interests, whether material or national. Thus, the communists embody the unbound multiplicity of consciousness, its anticipatory aspect, and therefore the precariousness of the bond, rather than its firmness. It is not for nothing that the maxim of the proletarian is to have nothing to lose but his chains, and to have a world to win. It is the bond that we must terminate, and what needs to come about is nothing but the affirmative multiplicity of capacities, whose emblem is polyvalent man, who undoes even those secular connections that bring together intellectual workers on the one hand, and manual workers on the other. And there is certainly no politics worthy of the name that doesn't propose, if not programmatically, then at least as a maxim, to have done with these connections.

From Lenin I retain the notions of 'iron discipline' and of the 'professional revolutionary'. An entire post-Leninist mythology – Stalinist in its formulation – exalts the supreme bond which unites the militant to the party and its leaders, and claims to find the source of politics in the aforementioned party. But the reality is that Lenin's party, the party of 1917, besides having been a disparate coalition riddled with all sorts of public disagreements, debates and factions, was held in very low esteem by Lenin himself in respect of the immediate demands of the situation. Lenin did not hesitate for a single second to contemplate resigning from the party – which, at the time, he showered with insults and denounced as a historical nonentity – when the party, privileging the bond of its continued existence over the risk that was posed to it, retreated, terrified, when the hour of insurrection was at hand.

Yet if, following Lazarus, one engages in a close reading of *What is to be done?*, which is ordinarily taken to provide the blueprint for the exclusive, self-sufficient party, one will see that the latter is entirely inferred from the demands of political vision, and that it is politics which subsumes organisational considerations, never the reverse. In the Leninist conception of politics, the necessity of formal discipline is grounded only in the situation's historical irregularities, and on the infinite diversity of singular tasks.

That being said, if party discipline is genuinely political (as opposed to being the network of interests responsible for socialising a State bureaucracy) does it, strictly speaking, constitute a bond? I seriously doubt it, and this doubt is, for me, the product of experience. For the real substance of political discipline is quite simply the discipline of processes. If you have to be on time for an early morning meeting with two factory workers, it is not because the internalised superego of the organisation assigns you to this task, nor because the social, or even convivial, power of the bond renders you susceptible to the perverse charm of tedious obligations. It is because, if you don't, you lose the thread of the process through which generic singularities partake of your own experience. And if you are obliged not to indulge in frivolous gossip about your political practices while attending a dinner party, this is not because of some ineffable, masochistic relation that ties you to your organisation. It is because the normal social bond that encourages you to be effusive muddies the clarity of unbindings which, at the furthest remove from irresponsible commentary, you work away at with the same professional precision as a scientific researcher (just as this researcher will not deem this dinner party the most appropriate place to detail the mathematico-experimental dimensions of his problem).

A genuinely political organisation, or a collective system of conditions for bringing politics into being, is the least bound place of all. Everyone on the ground is essentially alone in the immediate solution of problems, and their meetings, or proceedings, have as their natural content protocols of delegation and inquest whose discussion is no more convivial or superegotistical than that of two scientists involved in debating a very complex question.

Anyone who considers the agreement on truth resulting from such debates intrinsically in terms of terror will prefer the mildness of the bond and the cushion of scepticism. One shouldn't blame politics for what is, in actual fact, the result of a personal preference for the bound outpouring of the ego. By contrast, true instances of politics tend to manifest this faint coldness that involves precision.

Ultimately, what true politics undermines is the illusion of the bond, whether it be trade unionist, parliamentary, professional or convivial. Organised in anticipation of surprises, diagonal to representations, experimenting with lacunae, accounting for infinite singularities, politics is an active thought that is both subtle and dogged; one from which the material critique of all forms of presentative correlation proceeds, and which, operating on the edge of the void, calls on homogeneous multiplicities against the heterogeneous order of the State which claims to prevent their appearance.

It has always seemed paradoxical to me that this order would want to call itself 'democracy'. Obviously, it is a word that encapsulates a complex history, and the benefits it harbours cannot be dismissed just like that. But its obvious polysemy invites us to question the extent to which it can still be useful in philosophy. Or rather: can 'democracy', conditioned by modern instances of politics, be a metapolitical concept?

5

A Speculative Disquisition on the Concept of Democracy

Today the word 'democracy' is the principal organiser of consensus. It is a word that supposedly unites the collapse of the socialist States, the putative well-being enjoyed in our countries and the humanitarian crusades of the West.

In fact, the word 'democracy' concerns what I shall call *authoritarian opinion*. It is forbidden, as it were, not to be a democrat. More precisely, it stands to reason that humanity aspires to democracy, and any subjectivity suspected of not being democratic is regarded as pathological. At best it refers to a patient re-education, at worst to the right of military intervention by democratic paratroopers.

Thus democracy necessarily elicits the philosopher's critical suspicion precisely insofar as it falls within the realm of public opinion and consensus. Since Plato, philosophy has stood for a rupture with opinion, and is meant to examine everything that is spontaneously considered as *normal*. If 'democracy' names a supposedly normal state of collective organisation or political will, then the philosopher demands that we examine the norm of this normality. He will not allow the word to function within the framework of authoritarian opinion.

Everything consensual is suspicious as far as the philosopher is concerned.

Opposing the self-evident democratic ideal to the singularity of a politics, and particularly of a revolutionary politics, is a tried and tested tactic. It was already being used against the Bolsheviks long before the October Revolution of 1917. In fact, the accusation that Lenin's politics were undemocratic recalls a founding political criticism. And it is still quite interesting today to see how Lenin responded to it.

Lenin had two ways of countering this accusation. The first was to distinguish, in accordance with the logic of class analysis, two types of democracy: bourgeois democracy and proletarian democracy, and to maintain that the second will prevail, in terms of both its scope and its intensity, over the first.

But Lenin's second way of responding appears to me to be more appropriate to the way in which the question presently stands. He insists that *democracy* should in truth always be understood as *a form of State*. 'Form' means a particular configuration of the separate character of the State and of the formal exercise of sovereignty. In declaring democracy to be a form of State, Lenin enters into the filiation of classical political thought, including that of Greek philosophy, which declares that 'democracy' must ultimately be thought as a figure of sovereignty or power: the power of the demos or the people; the capacity of the demos to exert coercion for itself.

If democracy is a form of State, what strictly philosophical use is this category destined to have? For Lenin, the aim or idea of politics is the withering away of the State, the classless society, and therefore the disappearance of every form of State, including, quite obviously, the democratic form. This is what one might call generic communism, whose principle is provided by Marx in the *1844 Manuscripts*. Generic communism designates an egalitarian society of free association between polymorphous labourers where activity, rather than being governed by status and social or technical specialisations, is governed by the collective mastery of necessities. In such a society, the State as an authority separate from public coercion is dissolved. Politics, which is the expression of the interests of social groups, and whose aim is the conquest of power, is itself dissolved.

Thus, every communist politics strives for its own disappearance by striving to abolish the separate form of the State in general, even the State that declares itself to be democratic.

If one now represents philosophy as that which designates, legitimates or evaluates the ultimate aims of politics, or the regulatory ideas of political presentation; if one admits, as Lenin's hypothesis does, that the ultimate aim is the withering away of the State, otherwise known as pure presentation, or free association; or again, if the ultimate aim of politics is said to be the in-separate authority of the infinite, or collective self-realisation as such, then, in respect of this supposed aim – which is *the* designated aim of politics as generic communism – 'democracy' neither is, nor can it be, a philosophical category. Why? Because democracy is a form of the State; because philosophy evaluates the ultimate aims of politics; and because this aim is also for the end of the State, and so too the end of all relevance for the word 'democracy'.

In terms of this hypothetical framework, the only adequate *philosophical* word for evaluating the political is possibly the word 'equality', or 'communism', but certainly not the word 'democracy'. For this word remains bound by tradition to the State and to the form of the State.

What this entails is that 'democracy' can only become a philosophical concept if we give up one of three closely related hypotheses underlying the Leninist vision of the problem of democracy. Let us recall what they are:

Hypothesis 1. The ultimate aim of politics is generic communism, thus the pure presentation of the truth of the collective, or the withering away of the State.

Hypothesis 2. The relation of philosophy to politics consists in evaluating, in giving a general or generic meaning to, the ultimate aims of a politics.

Hypothesis 3. Democracy is a form of the State.

According to these three hypotheses 'democracy' is not an essential philosophical concept. Therefore it can only become so if at least one of these hypotheses is abandoned.

Three abstract possibilities are then opened up:

1. That the ultimate aim of politics is not generic communism.

2. That the relation philosophy has to politics does not consist in scrutinising, clarifying or legitimating its ultimate aims.

3. That 'democracy' designates something other than a form of the State.

Thus, our original starting point, according to which there are no grounds for recognising 'democracy' as a philosophical concept, is put in question and needs to be reexamined in light of at least one of these three conditions. I would therefore like to analyse, one by one, the three conditions under which 'democracy' can either begin or resume being a category of philosophy proper.

Let us suppose that the ultimate aim of politics is not the pure affirmation of collective presentation; that it is not the free association of men, unburdened of the principle of State sovereignty. Let us suppose that its ultimate aim, even as an idea, is not generic communism. So what can the aim, the purpose of political practice be, inasmuch as this practice concerns, questions or challenges philosophy?

I believe we can draw up two main hypotheses on the history of this question. According to the first, the aim of politics would be the configuration or the advent of what I shall agree to call the 'good State'. Philosophy would be an examination of the legitimacy of the State's different possible forms. It would seek to name the preferred figure of the statist configuration. Such would be the ultimate stake in the debate on the aims of politics. In fact, this approach continues the great classical tradition of political philosophy which, since the Greeks, has governed the question of sovereign legitimacy. At this point it is natural that a norm should emerge. Whatever the regime or status of this norm, an axiological preference for such and such a statist configuration relates the State to a normative principle which judges, for example, that the democratic regime is superior to the monarchist or aristocratic regime by invoking a general system of norms prescribing this preference.

Let us observe in passing that the same does not apply to the thesis according to which the ultimate aim of politics is the withering away of the State, precisely because the latter does not involve the good State. Instead what is at stake is not the conjunction of a norm and the statist figure, but the political process as self-termination, or the idea of a process that would carry out the withering away of the figure of the State by terminating the principle of sovereignty. The notion of 'withering away' is not part of the normative question about the persistence of the State. On the other hand, if the ultimate aim of politics is the good State, or the preferred State, then the emergence of a norm is inescapable.

And yet this question is difficult because the norm is inevitably external or transcendent. Considered in itself, the State is an objectivity without norm. It is the principle of sovereignty, or coercion, functioning separately, essential for the collective as such. It comes to acquire its determination through a prescription stemming from subjectifiable themes which are precisely the norms through which the question of the preferred State, or the good State, is arrived at. In our present situation, or the situation of our parliamentary States, one sees that the subjective relation to the question of the State is governed by three norms: the economy, the national question and, precisely, democracy.

Let us consider the economy first of all. The State is accountable for a minimum upkeep of circulation and distribution of goods, and is discredited as such if it proves excessively inept at fulfilling this norm. From the perspective of the economic sphere in general, and irrespective of the economy's organic relation to the State (private, public, etc.), the latter is subjectively accountable for the running of the economy.

The second norm is national. The State falls under the prescription of data such as the nation, how it is represented on the world stage, national independence, etc. It is accountable for the existence of the national principle both at home and abroad.

Third, democracy today itself constitutes a norm, one which is taken into account through its subjective relation to the State. The State can be held to account by being asked whether it is democratic or despotic, or by being asked about its relation to phenomena such as freedom of opinion, association and movement. The opposition between the dictatorial form and the democratic form is something that functions as a subjective norm in evaluating the State.

Overall, this question currently submits the State to the normative threefold arrangement of economic management, national assessment and democracy. In this situation, 'democracy' acts as a normative characterisation of the State, and more precisely as what might be called the category of *a* politics, rather than of *politics* in general. Here we take *a* politics to mean the regulation of a subjective relation to the State. And let us say that the statist figure which regulates this subjective relation under the three aforementioned norms – the economic, the national, the democratic – is what we are able to call parliamentarianism (personally I prefer to call it capital-parliamentarianism). However, since 'democracy' is invoked here as the category of a singular politics whose universality is known to be problematic, it will not qualify as being, in itself, a philosophical category. At this stage of the analysis I shall maintain that 'democracy' appears as a category which singularises, by means of the constitution of a subjective norm of the State relation, a particular politics that needs to be named and which I propose to designate as 'parliamentarianism'.

So much for the hypothesis that politics aims to determine the good State. What we end up with, at best, is 'democracy' as the possible category of a particular politics – parliamentarianism – which provides no decisive reason why 'democracy' should be retrieved, captured as a philosophical concept.

Let us recall that we began by considering what the ultimate aim of politics might be apart from generic communism. Our initial view was that politics aims to establish the best possible State. The conclusion is that 'democracy' is not necessarily a philosophical concept.

The second possible view is that politics has no aim other than itself. In this case politics would no longer be governed by the question of how to bring about the good State, but would instead be an end in itself. Contrary to what was previously maintained, politics conceived in this way would, in a certain manner, be the movement of thought and action that frees itself from dominant statist subjectivity and that proposes, summons and organises projects that cannot be reflected or represented by those norms under which the State operates. One could also say that, in this case, politics is presented as a singular collective practice operating at a distance from the State. Or again, that, in essence, politics is not the bearer of a State programme or a statist norm, but is rather the development of a possible affirmation as a dimension of collective freedom which subtracts itself from the normative consensus that surrounds the State, even if, quite obviously, this organised freedom pronounces its own verdict on the State.

So, can 'democracy' be relevant? Yes, I shall say so, *as long as 'democracy' is grasped in a sense other than a form of the State*. If politics is an end in itself by virtue of the distance it is able to take from the statist consensus, it might eventually be termed democratic. However, in this case the category would no longer operate in the Leninist sense as a form of State, which leads us back to the third negative condition of our three Leninist hypotheses.

This concludes the first part of our examination, namely: what if the aim of politics is not generic communism?

The second part concerns philosophy itself. Let us put forward the hypothesis that philosophy's relation to politics is not one of representation or the seizure of its ultimate aims; let us propose that philosophy's relation to politics is something different, and that this relation is neither the appraisal of ultimate aims, nor their appearance before a critical tribunal, nor their legitimation. What, then, is philosophy's relation to politics, and how are we to name or prescribe it? There is a first hypothesis, which is that the task of philosophy consists in what I would call the formal description of instances of politics, their typology.

Philosophy would constitute a discussion space for these instances by locating their different types. Overall, philosophy would be a formal apprehension of States and instances of politics by exposing and pre-elaborating the types in question in accordance with possible norms. But when this is the case – and indubitably it is one aspect of the work of thinkers such as Aristotle or Montesquieu – the fact is that, even in philosophy, 'democracy' appears to function as the name for a form of State. There is no doubt about it. The classification starts out from statist configurations and 'democracy' once more becomes, even from the philosophical perspective, the designation of a form of the State which stands opposed to other forms such as tyranny, aristocracy, etc.

But if 'democracy' designates a form of State, everything comes to depend, with regard to this form, on how the *aims of politics* are conceived. Is it a question of *requiring* this form? If so, then we remain within the logic of the good State, and we revert back to the question examined above. Is it a question of going beyond this form, of dissolving sovereignty, even democratic sovereignty? In this case we revert back to the Leninist framework whose hypothesis is the withering away of the State. In either case, this option leads us back to the first part of our examination.

The second possibility is the attempt by philosophy to grasp politics as a singular activity of thought whose apprehension, within the historico-collective domain, itself provides a form of thought that philosophy must seize as such. Here philosophy – consensually defined – is understood to mean the apprehension in thought of the conditions for the practice of thought in its different registers. If politics is the practice of a thought in an absolutely self-sufficient register (here one recognises the central thesis of Lazarus), then we can say that philosophy's task is to seize the conditions for the practice of thought within this singular register known as politics. In this case, then, I will make the following claim: if politics is a thought, and to the extent that it is, then it is impossible for it to be governed by the State, it cannot be conceived through or reduced to its statist dimension. Let us venture a slightly hybrid formula: *The State does not think*.

In passing, the fact that the State does not think is the source of all sorts of difficulties for philosophical thought about politics. One can demonstrate how all the 'political philosophies' (and this is why we must abandon their project) confirm the fact that the State does not think. And when these political philosophies attempt to take their bearings from the State in the investigation of politics as thought, the difficulties proliferate. The fact that the State does not think leads Plato, at the end of Book IX of the *Republic*, to declare as a last resort that politics can be done everywhere, except in his own country. This is also what leads Aristotle to the distressing observation that once the ideal types of politics have been isolated, it is notable how all that remain in reality are pathological ones. For example, for Aristotle monarchy is a State which thinks, and which is thinkable. But, in reality, there are only tyrannies that do not think and are unthinkable. The normative type is never realised. This also leads Rousseau to observe that throughout history there have only ever been dissolved States, but not one legitimate State. Finally, these statements, which are drawn from extremely varied political conceptions, agree on one point: namely, that it is not possible for the State to serve as a way in to the investigation of politics, at least not if politics is a thought. One inevitably comes up against the State as non-thought, which requires us to approach things from a different angle.

Consequently, if 'democracy' is a category of politics as thought, or if it is necessary for philosophy to utilise this category in order to seize the political process as such, this political process is perceptively subtracted from the pure prescription of the State, because the State itself does not think. It follows that 'democracy' is not to be grasped here as a form of the State, but in an altogether different sense. We are thus referred back to problem number 3.

One is then able to advance a provisional conclusion: 'democracy' is a category of philosophy only when it designates something other than a form of the State. But what?

Here, in my opinion, lies the heart of the question. It is a problem of conjunction. To what, apart from the State, must 'democracy' be conjoined in order to provide true access to politics as thought? Quite obviously this question assumes a considerable political legacy which there can be no question of detailing here. I will simply provide two examples of how the attempt to conjoin 'democracy' to something other than the State might serve a metapolitical (philosophical) reexamination of politics as thought.

The first attempt would be to conjoin 'democracy' directly to mass political activity; not to the statist configuration, but to that which is most immediately antagonistic to it. For mass political activity, or the spontaneous mobilisation of the masses, generally comes about through an anti-statist drive. This has provided the syntagm, romantic in my view, of mass democracy, and of the opposition between mass democracy and formal democracy, or democracy as a figure of the State.

Whoever has experience of mass democracy – in other words, historical phenomena such as general collective assemblies, mass gatherings, riots and so forth – will obviously recognise an immediate point of reversibility between mass democracy and mass dictatorship. The essence of mass democracy actually yields a mass sovereignty, and mass sovereignty is a sovereignty of immediacy, thus of the gathering itself. We know that the sovereignty of the gathering exerts a terroristic-fraternity in the modalities of what Sartre termed the 'group-in-fusion'. Sartrean phenomenology remains incontestable on this point. There is an organic correlation between the practice of mass democracy as an internal principle of the group-in-fusion and a point of reversibility with the immediately authoritarian or dictatorial element at work in terroristic-fraternity. If one examines this question of mass democracy for itself one will see that it is impossible to legitimate the principle in the name of democracy alone, for this romantic democracy immediately includes, both empirically and conceptually, its own reversibility into dictatorship. We are thus faced with a democracy/dictatorship dyad that resists elementary designation, or philosophical apprehension, under the sole concept of democracy. What does this mean? It means that whoever attributes a legitimacy to mass democracy, nowadays at any rate, does so on the horizon, or setting out from the horizon, of the non-statist perspective of pure presentation. The valorisation of mass democracy as such, even in the name of democracy, is inseparable from the subjectivity of generic communism. This dyad of democratic and dictatorial immediacy can only be legitimated to the extent that one thinks it, and valorises it, from the generic point of the disappearance of the State itself, or while setting out from radical anti-statism. In fact, the practical pole that confronts the consistency of the State, which is brought out precisely in the immediacy of mass democracy, is a provisional representative of generic communism itself. This leads us back to the questions resulting from our first major hypothesis: if 'democracy' is conjoined to *mass*, one indeed presumes that the aim of politics is generic communism, from which it follows that 'democracy' is not a philosophical category. This conclusion is empirically and conceptually borne out by the fact that on the question of mass democracy it is impossible to distinguish democracy from dictatorship. This is obviously what has enabled Marxists to hold on to the possibility of using the expression 'dictatorship of the proletariat'. However, it is important to understand that what facilitated the subjective valorisation of the word 'dictatorship' was precisely the existence of points of reversibility between democracy and dictatorship which assumed the historical figure of mass democracy, or revolutionary democracy, or romantic democracy.

There remains another, altogether different hypothesis for which it would be necessary to conjoin 'democracy' to the political prescription itself. 'Democracy' would in this case refer neither to the figure of the State nor to that of mass political activity, but would refer organically to the political prescription, under our present hypothesis that the latter is not governed by the State, or by the good State, and so is not programmatic. 'Democracy' would be organically bound to the universality of the political prescription, or to its universal capacity, which would establish a bond between the word 'democracy' and politics as such. Once again, politics would be something other than a State programme. This would allow for an intrinsically democratic characterisation of politics to the extent that, quite obviously, politics would be self-determined as a space of emancipation subtracted from the consensual figures of the State.

There is some evidence of this in Rousseau's work. In Chapter 16 of Book III of the *Social Contract*, Rousseau examines the question of the establishment of government – apparently the opposite question to the one which concerns us here – or the question of establishing a State. There he comes up against a well-known difficulty, namely that the act of establishing a government cannot be a contract, cannot concern the space of the social contract in the sense of founding the people as such, since the institution of a government concerns particular persons, and therefore cannot be a law. For, in Rousseau's estimation, a law is by necessity a global relation of the people to itself, and cannot designate particular persons. The institution of government cannot be a law. This means that it cannot be a sovereign exercise either. For sovereignty is precisely the generic form of the social contract, and is always a relation of totality to totality, of the people to itself. We seem to find ourselves in an impasse. It is important for there to be a decision which is both particular (since it sets up the government) and general (since it is taken by *all* the people, and not by the government, which doesn't yet exist, and which has to be instituted). However, in Rousseau's estimation it is impossible that this decision concerns the general will, since all decisions of this type must be presented in the form of a law, or through an act of sovereignty which can only be the contract passed from all the people to all the people, and which cannot have a particular character. One can also pose the problem in this way: the citizen passes laws, the governmental magistrate enacts particular decrees. How can one appoint particular magistrates when there are not yet magistrates, but only citizens? Rousseau emerges from this difficulty by stating that the institution of government is the result of 'a sudden conversion of Sovereignty into democracy ... by virtue of a new relation of all to all, [whereby] the citizens become magistrates and pass from general to particular acts'.[1] Many people have wryly remarked that this amounts to a very clever sleight of hand on Rousseau's part. What does this sudden conversion which leaves the organic relation of totality to totality unaltered mean? How does a mere displacement of this relation, which is the social contract constituting the general will, allow us to proceed to the possibility of carrying out particular political acts? If we put aside the formal argument, basically it means that democracy is related from the beginning *to the particular character of the stakes of the political prescription.* Since it has particular stakes – and, in the final analysis, particular stakes are all it can have – the political prescription is constrained by democracy. The Rousseauian case of the institution of government is but one symbolic example. In more general terms, I shall say that the universality of the political prescription, being singularly subtracted from the State's authority, can only be deployed as such in accordance with particular stakes and, when deployed in such a manner, is required to assume the democratic figure simply in order to remain political. Here a primordial conjunction between democracy and politics is effectively implemented.

Democracy could thus be defined as that which authorises a placement of the particular under the law of the universality of the political will. In a certain way, 'democracy' names the political figures of the conjunction between particular situations and a politics. In this case, and in this case alone, 'democracy' can be retrieved as a philosophical category, as from now on it comes to designate what can be called the effectiveness of politics, or politics in its conjunction with particular stakes. Understood in this way politics is clearly freed from its subordination to the State.

If one wished to develop this point further one would demonstrate how, for philosophy, 'democracy' designates, through its conjunction with the political prescription as such, the seizure of a politics whose prescription is universal, but which is also capable of being conjoined to the particular in a form wherein situations are transformed in such a way as to rule out the possibility of any non-egalitarian statement.

This demonstration is slightly complex, and I can only provide a brief sketch of it here. Let us suppose that 'democracy' designates the fact that politics, in the sense of a politics of emancipation, does not have the State as its ultimate referent, but instead the particularity of people's lives, or people as they appear in the public space. It then follows that politics would only be able to retain its integrity [*rester elle-même*], or democratic credentials, on condition that it refused to treat this particularity in a non-egalitarian way. For if politics treats this particularity in a non-egalitarian way then it introduces a non-democratic norm – in the sense I originally spoke about – and defeats the conjunction, which means that it would no longer be in a position to treat the particular on the basis of the universal prescription. Politics would begin to treat it in a different way, and on the basis of a particular prescription. Now, it could be shown that every particular prescription results in politics being re-administered by the State and placed under its statist jurisdiction by duress. Consequently, I shall say that the word 'democracy', taken in the philosophical sense, thinks a politics to the extent that, in the effectiveness of its emancipatory process, what it works towards is the impossibility, in the situation, of every non-egalitarian statement concerning this situation. That this work is real results from the fact that these statements are, through the action of such a politics, not prohibited, but impossible, which is a different thing altogether. Prohibition is always a regime of the State; impossibility is a regime of the Real.

One can also say that democracy, as a philosophical category, is that which *presents equality*. Or again, democracy is what prevents any predicates whatsoever from circulating as political articulations, or as categories of politics which formally contradict the idea of equality.

I believe that this drastically limits the possibility of making political use of any type of *communitarian* designation under the aegis of democracy as a philosophical pretext. For the communitarian designation, or the question of identitarian assignation, relates to subsets which cannot be dealt with according to the idea of the impossibility of non-egalitarian statements.

Consequently, one could also say that 'democracy' is what regulates politics in respect of communitarian predicates, or predicates of subsets. Democracy is what maintains politics in the realm of universality proper to its destination. It is what guarantees that all nominations in terms of racial or sexual characteristics, or in terms of hierarchy and social status, or statements formulated in terms of problems such as 'there is an immigrant problem', will be statements that undo the conjunction of politics and democracy. 'Democracy' means that 'immigrant', 'French', 'Arab' and 'Jew' cannot be political words lest there be disastrous consequences. For these words, and many others, necessarily relate politics to the State, and the State itself to its lowest and most essential of functions: the non-egalitarian inventory [*décompte*] of human beings.

When all is said and done, the task of philosophy is to expose a politics to assessment. An assessment carried out not with reference to the good State, or to the idea of generic communism, but an intrinsic assessment, or for itself. Politics can be defined sequentially as that which attempts to create the impossibility of non-egalitarian statements relative to a situation, and as what can be exposed through philosophy, and by means of the word 'democracy', to what I would call a certain eternity. Let us say that it is by means of the word 'democracy' thus conceived, and through philosophy and philosophy alone, that a politics can be evaluated according to the criteria of the eternal return. Then politics is seized by philosophy, not simply as a pragmatic or particular avatar of the history of men, but by being connected to a principle of assessment that upholds without ridicule and without crime the fact that the return is foreseeable.

And in fact a very old, worn-out word designates philosophically those instances of politics which emerge victorious from this ordeal: it is the word 'justice'.

Note

1 Jean-Jacques Rousseau, *The Social Contract*, trans. G.D.H. Cole. London: Dent, 1968, Book III, ch. xvii.

6

Truths and Justice[1]

We must set out from the following premise: injustice is clear, justice is obscure. For whoever endures injustice is its indubitable witness. But who can testify for justice? There is an affect of injustice, a suffering, a revolt. But there is nothing to indicate justice, which presents neither spectacle, nor sentiment.

Must we resign ourselves, then, to saying that justice is the mere absence of injustice? Is it the empty neutrality of a double negation? I don't believe so. Nor do I believe that injustice sides with the perceptible, or with experience, or with the subjective; and that justice sides with the intelligible, or with reason, or with the objective. Injustice is not the immediate disorder of which justice would serve as the ideal order.

'Justice' is a philosophical word – at least if we leave aside, as one should, its juridical signification, which is entirely the preserve of the police and the magistracy. However, this philosophical word is conditioned; it is conditioned by politics. For philosophy knows that it is incapable of realising in the world the truths it testifies to. Even Plato knows that, for there to be justice, the philosopher must in all likelihood be king, but that such a possibility certainly does not depend on philosophy. What it depends upon is the irreducible complexity of political circumstances.

We shall call 'justice' that through which a philosophy designates the possible truth of a politics.

We know that the overwhelming majority of empirical instances of politics have nothing to do with truth. They organise a mixture of power and opinions. The subjectivity that animates them is that of demand and *ressentiment*, of the tribe and the lobby, of electoral nihilism and the blind confrontation of communities. Philosophy has nothing to say about any of this, because philosophy only thinks thought, whereas these instances are explicitly presented as non-thoughts. The only subjective element of any importance to them is self-interest.

Throughout history, certain instances of politics have had or will have a relation to a truth; a truth of the collective as such. These are rare, often brief attempts, but they constitute the only conditions under which philosophy is able to think.

These political sequences are singularities, they trace no destiny, they construct no monumental history. They must be designated, in the terminology proposed by Sylvain Lazarus that we have already commented on at length, as historical modes of politics in interiority. Yet philosophy does manage to discern a common trait within these discontinuous sequences: namely, the strictly generic humanity of the people engaged in them. In their principles of action, these political sequences take no account of any particular interests. They bring about a representation of the collective capacity on the basis of a rigorous equality between each of their agents.

What does 'equality' mean here? Equality means that the political actor is represented under the sole sign of the uniquely human capacity. Interest is not a uniquely human capacity. All living things have as their imperative for survival the pursuit of their own interests. Thought is the one and only uniquely human capacity, and thought, strictly speaking, is simply that through

which the human animal is seized and traversed by the trajectory of a truth. Thus, a politics worthy of being interrogated
by philosophy under the idea of justice is one whose unique
general axiom is: people think, people are capable of truth. It
is the strictly egalitarian recognition of the capacity for truth
that Saint-Just had in mind when, in April 1794, he defined
public consciousness before the Convention: 'Embrace the
public consciousness, for all hearts are equal in terms of their
capacity to distinguish between good and evil, and this public
consciousness is constituted by the people's propensity towards
the general good.'[2] And we encounter the same principle, in an
entirely different political sequence, during the Cultural
Revolution in China. Thus, for example, in the Sixteen Points
of 8 August 1966: 'Let the masses educate themselves in this
great revolutionary movement, let them learn to distinguish
between the just and the unjust, between correct and incorrect
ways of doing things.'[3]

And so a politics touches on truth provided that it is founded
upon the egalitarian principle of a capacity to discern the just,
or the good, which are expressions that philosophy apprehends
under the aegis of the truth that the collective is capable of.

It is very important to note that 'equality' signifies nothing
objective here. It is not a question of the equality of social status,
income, function and still less of the supposedly egalitarian
dynamics of contracts or reforms. Equality is subjective. For
Saint-Just, what is at stake is equality with regard to public consciousness, while for Mao Tse-tung it is the equality of the
political mass movement. Such equality is by no means a social
programme. Moreover, it has nothing to do with the social. It
is a political maxim, a prescription. Political equality is not what
we desire or plan; it is that which we declare to be, here and
now, in the heat of the moment, and not something that should

be. Similarly, 'justice' cannot be, for philosophy, a State programme. 'Justice' is the qualification of an egalitarian moment
of politics *in actu*.

The trouble with most doctrines of justice is their will to define
what it is, followed by attempts to realise it. But justice, which is
the philosophical name for the egalitarian political maxim,
cannot be defined. For equality is not an objective of action, it
is its axiom. There is no politics bound to truth without the affirmation – an affirmation which can neither be proved nor
guaranteed – of a universal capacity for political truth. Where
truth is concerned, thought cannot adhere to the scholastic path
of definitions. It must proceed via the understanding of an axiom.

'Justice' is simply one of the words through which a philosophy attempts to *seize* the egalitarian axiom inherent in a genuine
political sequence. And this axiom is itself provided by singular
statements which are characteristic of the sequence, such as
Saint-Just's definition of public consciousness, or Mao's thesis
concerning the immanent self-education of the revolutionary
mass movement.

Justice is not a concept for which we would have to track down
more or less approximate realisations in the empirical world.
Conceived as an operator for seizing an egalitarian politics,
which is the same thing as a *true* politics, justice identifies a
subjective figure that is effective, axiomatic, immediate. It is
what makes Samuel Beckett's surprising assertion in *How It Is*
so profound: 'in any case we have our being in justice[,] I have
never heard anything to the contrary'.[4] Justice, which seizes the
axiom latent in a political subject, necessarily designates what
is, rather than what should be. Either the egalitarian axiom is
present in political statements, or it is not. Consequently, either
we are in justice, or we are not. Which also means: either
there is politics – in the sense in which philosophy encounters

political thought internally – or there is not. But if there is, and we are immanently related to it, then we are in justice.

Every definitional and programmatic approach to justice makes it into a dimension of State action. But the State has nothing to do with justice, for the State is not a subjective and axiomatic figure. The State, as such, is indifferent or hostile to the existence of a politics that touches on truths. The modern State aims only at fulfilling certain functions, or fashioning a consensus of opinion. Its subjective dimension merely consists in transforming, in resignation or *ressentiment*, Capital's economic necessity, or its objective logic. This is why every programmatic or statist definition of justice changes it into its opposite: justice becomes a matter of harmonising the interplay of conflicting interests. But justice, which is the theoretical name for an axiom of equality, necessarily refers to a wholly disinterested subjectivity.

This can be stated simply in the following terms. Every politics of emancipation, or any instance of politics which prescribes an egalitarian maxim, is an instance of thought *in actu*. But thought is the specific mode through which a human animal is traversed and overcome by a truth. Within such a subjectification, the limit of interest is crossed in such a way that the political process itself becomes indifferent to it. It is therefore necessary, as is borne out by all those political sequences with which philosophy is concerned, that the State be unable to recognise anything relevant to it in such a process.

The State, in its being, is indifferent to justice. Conversely, every politics which is a thought *in actu* entails, in proportion to its force and tenacity, serious trouble for the State. This is why political truth always shows up in moments of trial and turmoil. It follows that justice, far from being a possible category of statist and social order, is the name for those principles at work in rupture and disorder. Even Aristotle, whose aim is a fiction of political stability, declares at the beginning of Book 5 of *Politics*: 'Everywhere, those who seek equality revolt.'[5]

But Aristotle's conception remains statist, his idea of equality remains empirical, objective, definitional. The genuine philosophical statement would instead be: political statements bearing truth spring up in the absence of any statist and social order.

The latent egalitarian maxim is heterogeneous to the State. Thus, it is always in the midst of turmoil and disorder that the subjective imperative of equality is affirmed. What philosophy names 'justice' seizes the subjective order of a maxim through the inescapable disorder to which the State of interests is then exposed.

Finally, what does making a philosophical pronouncement on justice, here and now, amount to?

First of all, it is a matter of knowing which singular politics to adhere to, of knowing which one involves a thought worthy of being seized through the resources of the philosophical apparatus, of which the word 'justice' is but one of the components.

In today's confused and chaotic world, at a time when Capital seems to be triumphing through its own weakness, and when the so-called 'New World Order' [*politique unique*] seems to have achieved a miserable fusion of what is and what can be, this is no mean feat. To identify the rare sequences through which a political truth is constructed, without allowing oneself to become discouraged by capitalist-parliamentarian propaganda, is in itself a stringent intellectual discipline. What is even more difficult is to attempt, in the realm of 'doing politics', to be faithful to some axiom of equality by unearthing those statements that characterise our era.

It then becomes a matter of seizing the past or present manifestations of the politics in question philosophically. The task, then, is twofold:

1. To examine political statements along with their prescriptions, and draw from them their egalitarian kernel of universal signification.

2. To transform the generic category of 'justice' by putting it to the test of these singular statements, according to the always irreducible mode through which they carry and inscribe the egalitarian axiom in action.

Finally, it is a matter of showing that, thus transformed, the category of justice designates the contemporary figure of a political subject. It is this figure that enables philosophy to carry out, under its proper names, the eternal inscription that our time is capable of.

This political subject has gone under various names. He used to be referred to as a 'citizen', certainly not in the sense of the elector or town councillor, but in the sense of the Jacobin of 1793. He used to be called 'professional revolutionary'. He used to be called 'grassroots militant'. We seem to be living in a time when his name is suspended, a time when we must find a new name for him.

In other words, even by drawing on a history, albeit without continuity or concept, of what 'justice' was once able to designate, we still have no clear idea of what this word means today. Granted, we seem to have an abstract idea of what it means, since 'justice' always signifies the philosophical seizure of a latent axiom of equality. But this abstraction is useless. For the imperative of philosophy is to seize the event of truths, their novelty, their precarious trajectory. It is not the concept that philosophy directs towards eternity as the common feature of all thought, it is the singular process of a contemporary truth. A philosophy attempts to ascertain whether its own time is capable of upholding without ridicule or scandal the hypothesis of its own eternal return.

Is the contemporary state of politics such that philosophy can engage the category of justice therein? Or is any such suggestion merely to risk confusing chalk with cheese by reproducing the vulgar pretension of governments who presume to be able to dispense justice? When we see so many so-called 'philosophers' attempting to appropriate statist schemes as intellectually impoverished as Europe, capitalist-parliamentarian democracy, freedom in the sense of pure opinion, or some disgraceful nationalism – when we see philosophy grovelling like this before the idols of the day – there is obviously cause for pessimism.

But then, after all, the conditions for the practice of philosophy have always been rigorous. Philosophical words have always been subject to misappropriation and distortion whenever these conditions were not maintained. In this century there have been intense political sequences that have inspired the faithful. Here and there, in as yet incomparable situations, a few statements surround the egalitarian axiom in an uncompromising and rebellious manner. Politics does exist, even in France, particularly the politics of the Organisation Politique of which I am a member (I only mention it here because of its existence as a subjective condition of philosophy, or at least of *my* philosophy).

The collapse of the socialist States has a positive dimension. It was, without doubt, a question of pure and simple collapse. No politics worthy of the name played the slightest part in it. And this political vacuity has not ceased to engender monsters ever since. But then these terrorist States personified the ultimate fiction of a justice endowed with the solidity of a body, a justice existing in the form of a governmental programme. For an attentive philosopher, this collapse verifies the absurdity of such a representation. It releases justice and equality from every fictional incorporation. It restores them to their status, at once volatile and obstinate, of free prescription, of thought acting through and towards a collective seized by its truth. The collapse of the socialist States teaches us that the paths of egalitarian politics do not pass through State power, that politics is a matter of immanent subjective determination, an axiom of the collective.

After all, from Plato's unfortunate Sicilian venture to Heidegger's circumstantial aberrations, through the passive relations between Hegel and Napoleon, and not forgetting Nietzsche's madness in claiming 'to break the history of mankind in two',[6] everything proves that philosophy should not attempt to take its cue from History. Rather it should be sought in what Mallarmé called 'restricted action', which is one possible name for the truly thought-provoking sequences of politics *in actu*.

In politics, let us strive to be militants of restricted action. In philosophy, let us strive to be those who eternalise the figure of this action through a categorical framework wherein the word 'justice' remains essential.

We have too often wished for justice to found the consistency of the social bond, whereas in reality it can only name the most extreme moments of inconsistency. For the effect of the axiom of equality is to undo the bonds, to desocialise thought, to affirm the rights of the infinite and the immortal against the calculation of interests. Justice is a wager on the immortal against finitude, against 'being towards death'. For within the subjective dimension of the equality we declare, nothing is of interest apart from the universality of this declaration, and the active consequences that arise from it.

'Justice' is the philosophical name for the statist and social inconsistency of all egalitarian politics. And it is here that we are able to join in the declarative and axiomatic vocation of the poem. For it is Paul Celan who probably provides us with the most precise image of 'justice' in the following poem, with which I am well and truly able to conclude:

> Support yourself
> by inconsistencies:
> two fingers
> snap in the abyss, in
> scribblebooks
> a world rushes up, this depends
> on you.[7]

Let us bear in mind the lesson of the poet: in matters of justice, where inconsistency provides the sole support, it is true, as true as a truth can be, that this depends on you.

For it is always in subjectivity, rather than the community, that the egalitarian edict [*l'arrêt*] interrupting and overturning the usual course of conservative politics is uttered.

At this point the focus of discussion moves to the metapolitical work of Jacques Rancière, one of whose fundamental nominations, conjoining what I have separated, is 'community of equals'. We shall examine Rancière's work in two phases: his work from the 1980s, whose main book is *The Ignorant Schoolmaster*; and his work from the 1990s, which culminates in *Disagreement*.

Notes

1 A version of this text was originally published as 'Vérités et justice' in Jacques Poulain ed., *Qu'est-ce que la justice?*, Saint-Denis: Presses Universitaires de Vincennes, 1996, pp. 275–81.

2 'Rapport au nom du Comité de Salut Public et du Comité de Sûreté Générale sur la police générale, sur la justice, le commerce, la législation et les crimes des factions, présenté à la Convention Nationale dans la séance du 26 Germinal An II', in *Oeuvres Complètes de Saint-Just*, Paris: Gérard Lebovici, 1984, p. 811.

3 'Decision of the CCP Central Committee Concerning the Great Proletarian Cultural Revolution', in *Documents of Chinese Communist Party Central Committee*. September 1956–April 1969, Vol. I, Hong Kong: Union Research Institute, 1971, p. 210. [*Translation modified.*]

4 Samuel Beckett, *How It Is*, trans. the author. London: John Calder, 1964, p. 135.

5 Aristotle, 'Politics', trans. Benjamin Jowett, *The Basic Works of Aristotle*, ed. R. McKeon. New York: Vintage, 2001, 1301b26. [*Translation modified.*]

6 The quotation is from F. Nietzsche, 'Why I Am a Destiny' in *Ecce Homo*, trans. Walter Kaufmann. New York: Vintage, 1969, para 8. *Trans.*

7 Paul Celan, 'An die Haltlosigkeiten', in *Zeitgehöft*, Frankfurt: Suhrkamp Verlag, 1976. Badiou's translation of the first two lines of the poem differs significantly from the version very kindly provided for the present edition by John Felstiner, which reads: 'Creeping up close/to lost footholds'. As such I have opted to modify the first two lines in order to retain more faithfully the explicit sense of Badiou's argument on the relation between inconsistency and justice. I am grateful to John Felstiner for permission to publish. *Trans.*

7

Rancière and the
Community of Equals

Rancière's doctrinal style can be characterised according to three imperatives: Always situate yourself in the interval between discourses without opting for any of them; reactivate conceptual sediments without lapsing into history; deconstruct the postures of mastery without giving up the ironic mastery of whosoever catches the master out.

The site for Rancière's enterprise is not internal to a system [*dispositif*] of knowledge, although he is capable of erudite scholarship and is a keen archivist. For the point at issue is never being a member, *ex officio*, of any particular academic community, whilst consistently drawing on textual positivities. In this regard, Rancière is an heir to Foucault – albeit without sharing the latter's Nietzschean postulates – whose approach consists in a rebellious apprehension of discursive positivities.

Is his book of 1981, *The Nights of Labor*,[1] a historian's archaeology of the figure of the proletarian? Or is it an ideological intervention aiming to establish the inconsistency of this figure as it had previously been handled by orthodox Marxism? Or again, are we confronted by a latent philosophy of time, discourse and the imaginary? Without doubt the book presents us with a memorial diagonal of the three options.

In his book of 1983, *The Philosopher and His Poor*,[2] we encounter a well-documented analysis of the 'people' as an abiding reference for theoretical speculations, both in terms of its staging and its cancellation. The title is a clear index of the anti-philosophical charge of this analysis. But ultimately the relation to the text exceeds exposure and tends, in an aporetic manner, towards a political intervention that is forever suspended.

In his very fine book of 1987, *The Ignorant Schoolmaster*,[3] we have the prototype for an exhumation of archives in that most astonishing figure of the anti-master, Jacotot. But the book is equally a fictional reconstruction of this figure aimed at facilitating a discussion on the equality of intellects.

In sum we can say that Rancière takes delight in occupying unrecognised spaces between history and philosophy, between philosophy and politics, and between documentary and fiction. To what ends?

If I say, borrowing Husserl's well-known expression, that what is at stake here is the reactivation of sediments, it will be to add in the same breath that this reactivation does not take place from within the phenomenological perspective of a discovery of meaning. Of course, Rancière is well versed at detecting abolished or diverted strata of statements which lie beneath established discourses. He sets himself the task of making their signifying [*signifiante*] energy circulate anew. But what he unearths is not, as in the case of Husserl, a primordial ground of meaning, a pre-predicative existence, a founding site [*un site fondateur*].[4] What he discovers is a discourse plotted and held in the aftermath of an event, a sort of social flash of lightning, a brief and local invention, both prior to and coextensive with domination and its burdens. This invention circulates horizontally rather than vertically, for it constitutes the surfacing of the latent force of the dominated, and amounts to a demonstration that this force, which in most cases is diverted from its true course, is what drives the machinations of the dominators.

In fact, the location of this horizontal line, of this scrawl witnessed on the fabric of history, is the historian's operator of the third function of Rancière's text: it undermines the postures of mastery, and the political or philosophical postures in particular.

Rancière never refutes anyone, for this would itself confirm the master's authority. Refutation establishes heritage, succession. In the great anti-philosophical tradition, Rancière wants instead to discredit the master by showing that his position suggests representations whose arrangement is fallacious. And the fact that it is fallacious is established precisely through the local expressions of the non-mastery of the dominated who contradict, at each and every moment, the guarantees of the master's existence. From this perspective there is, in Lacan's sense, a brilliant hysteria to Rancière, who singles out, towards the lowly end of the social universe, the always somewhat repugnant condition of the master's inaugural statement.

Rancière's singular constructions are essentially supported by two very simple theses:

1. All mastery is an imposture. Rancière thereby inscribes himself, in spite of everything, within the French anarchist and utopian tradition of old, of which he is both the second-generation thinker and the sympathetic, patient and ironic archivist.

But since he is attuned to the real refrain of the social world, and remains sensitive to what is beneficial in institutions, Rancière also maintains that:

2. Every bond presumes a master.

From these two theses a doctrine of equality is inferred, which is Rancière's true abstract passion, and whose axiom is that anyone, regardless of experience, can exert mastery without being in a position of mastery provided that the anyone in question is willing to be unbound.

It is at this point that the motif of the community of equals, on the basis of this nineteenth-century myth, undoubtedly places the most considerable demands on Rancière. For the community of equals is the hypothesis of a social bond set free from the imposture of the master, and therefore the realisation *in actu* of the latent contradiction between Rancière's two theses.

In dismantling this myth as a false *telos* of emancipatory politics, the paradox is that Rancière leads us to nothing in the order of real politics that could serve as a replacement.

The theme of the community of equals or, as Marx says, of 'free association' (and thus so too of the withering away of the State) suggests either a totality without master (this is his most clearly utopian version, openly contradicting Rancière's second thesis) or an equality which is held together under a pure empty mark of mastery, whose vertical absence provides the foundation for the horizontal bond (this is the idea of a shared mastery without a master position).

Let us observe that the supposed existence of a community of equals would destroy the very intellectual site (interval of discourses, reactivation of sediments, deconstruction of the master's position) that Rancière wishes to inhabit. For if the community of equals is realisable then there is no more interval, only what is unique and held in common; there is no more sediment, since communitarian self-affirmation eliminates all tradition, regarding it as ancient and foreclosed; and there is no longer any master position, since communitarian rites mean that everyone is the brother of everyone else.

Rancière thus proceeds to a critique of the communitarian motif as realisation in order to replace it with the idea of a declared and delineated 'moment' of equality conceived in its intrinsic bond with inequality. There is an impasse of the paradigm, and a retrospective promotion of the real flash of lightning, of the scrawling on the surface of time.

But this retrospection is deceptive, for by no means does it allow us to draw conclusions as to the possibility of politics, here and now. It seems to me that the deconstruction of the ideal of the community of equals functions in reality as a pure and simple verdict of a militant impossibility.

Rancière once told me that there are always more than enough people to draw conclusions and, moreover, the conclusions of those who do gravitate towards the general consensus. Here lies the correspondence, quite perceptible in all of Rancière's work, of a negative certainty and a suspense of the prescription, or of the conclusion. For him it is a question, at best, of fixing a peg, or a skilfully constructed paradox, on the general incline of premature conclusions. His books are neither conclusions nor directives, but *arrest clauses*. You will come to know what politics must not be, you will even know what it will have been and no longer is, but never what it is within the Real, and still less what one must do in order for it to exist.

But what if, in making this point, Rancière was doing nothing but repeating the essence of our times? What if, in political matters, this essence was simply that of *not* concluding, of prescribing nothing?

Let us accept that the dream of the community of equals, or generic communism as a militant aim, must be brought to an end. Let us accept that equality must always be posed as a

singular thesis, a localised articulation of the already-said and
of the being-able-to-say. Does it follow that it is impossible to
say what an organic and uncompromising politics is here and
now, whose equality would be, precisely, an axiom and not a
goal? In Rancière's thought what set of *consequences* ultimately
results from his own intervention?

As for the community of equals, or the socialised figure of
equality, Rancière leads the way in having established its paradigms, studied its rules, demonstrated its impasse. He has
strongly maintained that equality must be *postulated* and not
willed. The fact is that in our situation there are, chiefly, either
statements that imply the explicit negation of equality (let us call
them 'right-wing' statements) or statements which claim to will
equality programmatically (let us call them 'left-wing' statements). Both types of statement are opposed to whoever
postulates equality and pursues, not the desire for equality, but
the consequences of its axiom. No doubt it is not a question,
either for myself or Rancière, of claiming to establish in an
uncertain future the *reality* of equality, any more than it is to
deny its principle. In this sense let us say that we are neither of
the right nor of the left. But what one is perfectly able to will
and prescribe is the universal domination, or universal evidence,
of the egalitarian *postulation*. One can prescribe, case by case,
situation by situation, the *impossibility of non-egalitarian statements*.
For this impossibility alone, inscribed in the situation through a
protracted politics in the places that are peculiar to it, verifies
that equality is not at all realised, but *real*.

We must reach agreement on the claim that equality has
nothing to do with the social, or social justice, but with the
regime of statements and prescriptions, and is therefore the
latent principle, not of simple scrawls on the parchment of proletarian history, but of every politics of emancipation. Yes, there

can be, there is, here and now, a politics of equality, one which it isn't simply a matter of realising but, having postulated its existence, of creating here or there, through the rigorous pursuit of consequences, the conditions for a universalisation of its postulate.

Notes

1 Jacques Rancière, *The Nights of Labor: The Workers' Dream in Nineteenth-Century France*, trans. John Drury. Philadelphia: Temple University Press, 1989. [*La Nuit des prolétaires, Archives du rêve ouvrier*, Paris: Fayard, 1981.]

2 Jacques Rancière, *The Philosopher and His Poor*, trans. John Drury, Corinne Oster, Andrew Parker. Durham, NC: Duke University Press, 2004. [*Le Philosophe et ses pauvres*, Paris: Fayard, 1983.]

3 Jacques Rancière, *The Ignorant Schoolmaster. Five Lessons in Intellectual Emancipation*, trans. Kristin Ross. Stanford: Stanford University Press, 1991. [*Le Maître ignorant*, Paris: Fayard, 1987.]

4 An axial concept in Badiou's ontology which he defines as the point, 'on the edge of the void', below which nothing can exist; Alain Badiou, *L'Être et l'événement*, méditation seize. *Trans.*

8

Rancière and Apolitics

In *Disagreement*[1] Rancière pursues a complex undertaking because he attempts to weave together, with the addition of some new operators, all the essential motifs of his thought. Let us recall these motifs.

1. A subtle variation on the anti-Platonism of the twentieth century, an anti-Platonism shared by Rancière, who in so doing deploys his work in a sharply anti-philosophical tone. There was, we have said, a classist occurrence of this tone (*The Philosopher and His Poor*, or even the conviction, explicit in *La Leçon d'Althusser*,[2] that philosophers always draw their inspiration from a fictitious proletariat). In *Disagreement* Rancière proceeds a little differently. He opposes real politics (not the one we want, but the one that has taken place) to the politics of philosophers, or the politics of truth. He maintains that the politics of philosophers is inevitably undemocratic, a fact they are either aware of and admit (which is the paradoxical virtue of Plato) or, as is the case today, they imagine their politics to be more radically democratic than real politics. But, in this second case, political philosophy is in fact only the melancholic accompaniment of an absence of real politics, obscurely informing the desire to have done with politics altogether.

2. An egalitarian methodology which, as Rancière says, is 'the nonpolitical condition of politics'.[3] What Rancière calls 'politics' is not of the order of the prescription or the organised project. It is a historical occurrence of equality, its inscription, or its declaration. It is the axiom that affirms the equality of anyone and everyone that is exercised *within* inequality or the wrong.

3. A theory of the gap, considered in terms of an act of exclusion [*Une théorie de l'écart, comme mise à l'écart*]. Politics exists (in the sense of an occurrence of equality) because the whole of the community does not count a given collective as one of its parts. The whole counts this collective as nothing. No sooner does this nothing express itself, which it can do only by declaring itself to be whole, than politics exists. In this sense the 'we are nothing, let us be everything' of *The Internationale* sums up every politics (of emancipation, or equality).

4. A theory of names. Politics presupposes the sudden appearance of a name, in which case the nothing is counted as a gap [*écart*] between the whole and itself. This is the case with the name 'proletarian'. The downfall of a name, as with the political significance of the name 'worker' nowadays, amounts to a termination of the politics bound to this name. Rancière will say that our time is *nameless*. In this respect the community as a whole declares itself effectively total or without remainder, which means that it declares itself without politics.

Overall, Rancière's doctrine can be defined as a democratic anti-philosophy that identifies the axiom of equality, and is founded on a negative ontology of the collective that sublates the contingent historicity of nominations.

To begin with I can say, along with a few others, that I recognise myself in important parts of Rancière's work. And all the more so since I have the literally justifiable feeling of having largely anticipated, along with a few others, these parts.

As far as the notion of domination is concerned – or the counting of parts of a whole as substructure of the unequal – this I named not long ago, in my own jargon, 'the state of the situation' and Rancière names 'the police' (playing on the Greek word $\pi o\lambda \iota \varsigma$). That it is necessary – in order to think change – to think the correlation between the counting and non-counted, the State and insecurity (what I call the 'on the edge of the void'), between the all and nothing, is indeed my conviction. Everything hinges on the nominal summoning, through an event, of a sort of central void at the surface of a situation statified by a counting procedure.

One could say that our agreement on this question is ontological, except that Rancière takes no risk to ensure the speculative cohesion of the requisite categories (whole, void, nomination, remainder, etc.), and only instils them with a sort of historicist phenomenology of the egalitarian occurrence. Admittedly, no one is obliged, in order to do politics, to deploy an underlying ontology. It may even be advisable to do without one. But Rancière doesn't do politics. If, on the other hand, one does philosophy, there is an obligation to make use of explicit ontological categories and to argue their cohesion. However, all things considered, Rancière doesn't do philosophy either.

With regard to politics as occurrence or singularity, and never as structure or programme, Rancière ends up by saying that politics is a mode of subjectification. In this case I can only recall the theses, examined at the beginning of this book and deployed by Sylvain Lazarus some time ago, which announce that politics is of the subjective order, and is thought in terms of its rare and sequential existence. According to the category of 'historical mode', politics is an irreducibly singular thought.

I shall accept on this occasion that our agreement concerns the doctrine of singularities, except to say that Rancière's understanding of singularity, as pure historical occurrence, is not established in its internal consistency, and must be 'carried' as it were by the unequal or the State, or in other words by history. This is not the case with my thought of politics as a truth process, for singularity is determined in its being (this is its generic reality) and has no relation as such to historical time, for it constitutes its own time through and through.

As far as the declaratory dimension of politics is concerned, which proclaims its non-political condition (equality) within the space of inequality, our agreement is equally tenable. Indeed I believe that, in the field of politics, a declaration is the simultaneous eruption of a nomination of wrong on the one hand, and a previously invisible and fully affirmative subjective point on the other. I should at least report that in 1988 the Organisation Politique published a collection of worker, popular and student declarations touching on very diverse situations (in other words where the aforementioned wrong and subsequent affirmation involved disparate situations). Therefore we can only agree with Rancière when he argues that the declaration is fundamentally an identifiable form of politics.

As to the fact that politics makes visible the invisible peculiar to the state of the situation, I must say that there exist explicit political occurrences of this determination, often significantly prior to Rancière's historicist systematisation. Let us mention, for example, a conference held by the Organisation Politique dating back to 1987 whose title was, quite simply: 'The Invisibles'.

We should also add several agreements on points of conjuncture. For example, Rancière takes up the analysis, which we have

been proposing for a good while, according to which the main
function of the word 'immigrant' has been the abolition of the
word 'worker' from the field of politics. Moreover, from this perspective, it was an operation that drew complicity from all the
parliamentary parties, the outcome of this consensus being the
obliteration of the PCF by the Front National.

Similarly, Rancière demonstrates in the wake of my *Ethics*, to
which he refers amicably, that the mainspring of the efferves-
cent promotion of human rights and humanitarian interventions
is a political nihilism, and that its real aim is to have done with
the very idea of an emancipatory politics.

This shows the extent of the overlap. And yet as so often is
the case when everything appears similar, nothing really is. I
would like to set out the radical discord between us, which so
many similarities conceal, in four points.

1. To begin with, let us consider the relation of philosophy to
politics. Of course, there cannot be politics *in* philosophy, and
the project of a founding or reflexive 'political philosophy' is futile,
since it merely ratifies its ideological subordination to a real
politics (I have demonstrated as much in respect of the contemporary readings of Hannah Arendt's work, which in fact amount
to abstract promotions of parliamentarianism). But it by no
means follows that philosophy is disqualified on this question. I
previously mentioned that even Plato knows perfectly well that
for the philosopher to become king would require real political
circumstances intransitive to philosophy and that, therefore, what
he says about the city is in the final analysis conditioned by effective political processes. The correct thesis is that all philosophy
is conditioned by instances of politics, to which philosophy gives
shelter through a particular transcription destined to produce
strictly philosophical effects. The thesis cannot come down to a

formal opposition between politics (the just practice of equality within inequality) and philosophy (as melancholia of principles bearing on the absence of a 'true' politics).

2. Rancière takes up the idea, with little or no alteration, that power is above all the power of the counting of parts of the situation. This was the definition that I gave, in 1988, to the state of the situation, and it is the one that Rancière, in 1996, gives in his *Eleven Theses on Politics*[4] to what he calls the 'police', which is 'partition of the perceptible' and 'counting of parts of a society'. He even takes up the central idea of my ontology, i.e. that what the State strives to foreclose through its power of counting is the void of the situation, while the event always reveals it: the principle of the police, he says, is 'the absence of void and of supplement'. Very good! The initial consequences of this are that a real politics holds itself at a distance from the State and constructs this distance (Rancière's variants: 'politics is not the exercise of power', and 'politics is a specific rupture of the logic of *arkhe*'); after which, following Lazarus on this point, politics is rare and subjective (Rancière's variants: politics 'happens as an always provisional accident in the history of forms of domination', and its essence is 'the action of supplementary subjects inscribed as surplus in relation to any counting of parts of a society'). We couldn't repeat things any better than that ourselves.

However, one will observe that Rancière avoids the word 'State', preferring alternatives of the 'society' or 'police' type. Even less does he set out to consider the *actual* State, the one around which parties, elections and, finally, 'democratic' subjectivity are organised. This State remains unnamed through the singular exercise of the counting of parts, such as is practised today.

And yet, today, every real (non-philosophical) politics is first of all to be accounted for in terms of its verdicts on this State. It is quite paradoxical that Rancière's critical thought breaks off just before the qualification, in respect of the political supplement, of the parliamentary State. And I suspect that it is a question for Rancière of never exposing himself, whatever the trajectory of his argument, to the mortal accusation of not being a democrat.

Having endured the effects of this accusation for twenty years I can understand his speculative prudence. The trouble is that it is precisely here that the line of demarcation passes between the intellectual effectiveness of a free politics and the self-restraint of political philosophy. Moreover, to establish a distance from the State so that a few prescriptions concerning it are possible would of itself demand that one declares oneself foreign both to the parliamentary State and to electoral rite, as well as to the parties that are shaped by it. Short of bringing about the practice of such a declaration, Rancière transforms his reflections on the distance, the supplement, the interruption of counting and so on, into ideological motifs, which indicates that they are nothing if not purely and simply *compatible* with the logic of parliamentary parties. It is a bit like the way in which, throughout the final phase of their existence, the PCF and its Trotskyist satellites were able to handle the 'revolutionary' motif while merely mobilising their troops for the local elections. It is not possible, and Rancière's suspended enterprise proves it, to determine the formal conditions for a politics beyond the State without ever examining how the question is posed *for us*, whose task it is to pursue the question in respect of the parliamentary State.

3. Much of this is explained by the fact that Rancière shares the common idea of a retreat or an absence of politics, and yet

is willing to put this idea on trial when it comes to its philosophical consequences. Given that *Disagreement* concludes with strictly negative reflections, it is quite possible that Rancière wants to have done with politics *as well*. For neither the escalation of identity politics rendered amenable to consensus (which Rancière knows, as we do, includes the Front National) nor the politically radical experience of the inhuman is enough to 'found' any progressive politics whatsoever. Agreed! We expect nothing good or 'politically correct' from communities, or from the eternal shadow of Auschwitz. But so what? Is the capacity to deal with the egalitarian axiom within a situation, in singular statements, on this basis unworkable? Rancière borrows from the Organisation Politique one of its most important themes: that the word 'immigrant' has in fact served, in a consensual manner, first to conceal and then to drive out the word 'worker' from the space of political representations. But what he forgets to say is that if we were able to discern this logic it was because we were bound [*attachés*], in concrete factory-places, to the definition and political practice of a new use for the figure of the worker. For the identification of a politics (on this occasion the consensual will to eliminate all reference to the figure of the worker) is only achieved from the perspective of *another* politics. We thus find in Rancière the means for taking up political *results* by cutting them off from the processes that give rise to them. This practice ultimately relies upon what he himself highlights as a philosophical imposture: forgetting the real condition of one's speech.

4. Rancière fails to say that every political process, even in the sense in which he understands it, manifests itself as an *organised* process. He has the tendency to pit phantom masses against an unnamed State. But the real situation demands instead that we pit a few rare political militants against the

'democratic' hegemony of the parliamentary State: the stage on which the contest is being played out is far removed from the one on which Rancière is trying to describe it.

The central subjective figure of politics is the political militant, a figure totally absent from Rancière's system. Here we touch upon the most important debate of the late twentieth century: can politics still be thought in the form of the party? Is the political militant inevitably the party militant? The crisis of the communist parties, including their evolution into the party-State, is as yet no more than an indication. For the electoral and subjective mediation of parliamentary politics remains indubitably that of parties. It's all very well for the run-of-the-mill intellectual to deride political parties and their activists; they still receive his vote when he is asked to cast it. But when Le Pen's party gains parliamentary successes and begins to make inroads into the State, the intellectual is the first to whine about the weakness of the traditional conservative parties and the crisis in which they find themselves.

Rancière would no doubt agree with us that, ultimately, parties, entirely under State control, incapable of rigorous or innovative prescriptions, can only persist in their crisis. As we have been repeating for several years, the question worth highlighting is one of a politics *without party*, which in no sense means unorganised, but rather one organised through the intellectual discipline of political processes, and not according to a form correlated with that of the State. However, we must accept the consequences of this position and recognise that, on these questions, where no *a priori* deduction is possible and where history cannot help us, it is politics in its interior mode that enables us to identify what the idea of a politics without party involves.

Essentially, Rancière tends to identify politics in the realm of its absence, and from the effects of its absence. On this basis it becomes difficult for him truly to distinguish himself from political philosophy, against which he constantly rages. He is a bit like a magician who conjures up shadows. However, there is a shadow only because next to it, small as it is, there is a tree, or a shrub. It is a shame that Rancière knows of the existence of this political tree, and of its real pressure, but that in order not to disturb the dreary plain which surrounds it unduly, he stubbornly refuses to climb onto it.

No doubt he draws consolation by telling himself that, through this difficult exercise, and without paying the highest price, he managed to avoid being, like so many others, a renegade rallying to consensus, a Thermidorean.

Notes

1 Jacques Rancière, *Disagreement. Politics and Philosophy*, trans. Julie Rose. Minneapolis: University of Minnesota Press, 1999. [*La Mésentente. Politique et philosophie*, Paris: Galilée, 1995.]

2 Jacques Rancière, *La Leçon d'Althusser*, Paris: Gallimard, 1974.

3 Jacques Rancière, *Disagreement*, p. 61.

4 Jacques Rancière, *Eleven Theses on Politics*, lecture given on 4 December 1996 in Ljubljana (source: http://www.zrc-sazu.si/www/fi/aktual96/ranciere.htm).

What is a Thermidorean?[1]

It is widely held that the Terror was brought to an end by the 'parliamentary' plot of the 9 Thermidor, which was followed by the Thermidorean Convention. Nowadays, at a time when any emancipatory political project is tainted by 'the crimes of communism', such a view absolves and even endorses the Thermidorean intervention. In fact, I note that the chief author of the bestselling book about the aforementioned crimes justifies his project by reminding us that he himself used to be a Maoist militant twenty years ago.[2] All things considered, this bestseller amounts to his own personal Thermidor. The fact that it makes him a great deal of money in the process is as it should be: this is just what the Thermidoreans of 1794 would also have wanted.

Yet despite its deceptive simplicity, presupposing as it does a version of the history of the Revolution that is at once linear and periodised, this view is open to numerous objections. The Thermidorean Convention was itself founded on a terrorist massacre: Robespierre, Saint-Just and Couthon, along with nineteen others, were executed without trial on 10 Thermidor. On 11 Thermidor, the tumbril carried off seventy-one condemned, the biggest tally of the entire Revolution. The counter-revolutionary terror scarcely lets up during the years

1794 and 1795, whether in the form of legal executions or random massacres. There are armed gangs everywhere inciting Jacobin militants to violence so as to provoke further clampdowns. One document in particular is most revealing on this point: Duval's *Thermidorean Remembrances*.[3] Duval was one of the activists belonging to what was called the gilded youth of Fréron. The war cry of these hatchet men was: 'Down with the Jacobins'. Moreover, the closure of the Jacobin club came in the wake of a brawl initiated by Fréron's gangs, a classic example of a governmental provocation.

It is important to recall here that, for Saint-Just, political thought holds virtue as its subjective maxim, and that terror is only the occasional substitute for the precariousness of virtue whenever the counter-revolution is raging inside and out. This precariousness exposes the course of politics to corruption. Terror, which is the only guarantee against the weaknesses of virtue, the only durable force against corruption, must ultimately be replaced by institutions.

But what institutional practice do the Thermidoreans inaugurate? It is summed up by the constitution of Year III, in which it becomes apparent that virtue has been replaced by a statist mechanism upholding the authority of the wealthy, which amounts to reinstalling corruption at the heart of the State. The central principle is obviously a voting system based on the poll tax, where the voters are themselves appointed by active citizens: 30,000 voters for the entire country!

But the maxims of repression are even more interesting. For they expressly target every kind of popular *declaration* that situates itself at a distance from the State. Thus article 366 proclaims: 'Every unarmed gathering shall be dispersed.' Article 364 stipulates that petitions (protests) remain strictly individual: 'No association may present them collectively, except the constituted

authorities, and then only for matters within their jurisdiction.'
And article 361 goes so far as to regulate the functioning of adjec-
tives: 'No assembly of citizens may call itself a popular society.'[4]

Thermidor opens a sequence wherein constitutional repression is backed up by an anti-popular vision of the State. It is
not so much a question of ending the terror exerted over adver-
saries as of bringing about a radical shift in the source and target
of that terror. From now on its source is the State constituted
by rich, eligible voters; while its target is every will constituted
or assembled on the basis of a popular declaration. Thus, the
Constitution of Year III turns its back on the Constitution of
1793, until then unequalled in its democratic statements. The
Directory will subsequently pursue this path right up to the –
truly momentous – decision to sentence to death anyone daring
to invoke the Constitution of 1793!

As we can see, the empirical notion that the coup of 9
Thermidor brought about an 'end to the Terror' cannot be
sustained.

Can we say, then, that Thermidor is the point at which the
revolutionary sequence of 1792–94 is clarified, and from within
this sequence the moment when the Terror becomes 'the order
of the day'? This would be to regress to the logic of the dialectical result, to the dialectic of synthesis and the idea that the
truth of a political sequence is embodied in its future. This is
certainly how Soboul,[5] for example, examines the relationship
between the Thermidorean Convention and the dictatorship of
the great committees. For Soboul, the Jacobins were victims of
their own contradictions, and the synthesis that envelops
Thermidor, the Directory, the Consulate and the Empire brings
forth the truth of these contradictions: once let loose, the
Revolution's essentially bourgeois nature cannot but shatter its
illusory appearance as a popular uprising.

Against the notion of dialectical synthesis, it is necessary to invoke here Sylvain Lazarus' thesis that a political sequence should be identified and thought on its own terms, as a homogeneous singularity, and not in terms of the heterogeneous nature of its empirical future. Specifically, a political sequence does not terminate or come to an end because of external causes, or contradictions between its essence and its means, but through the strictly immanent effect of its capacities being exhausted. It is precisely this exhaustion that Saint-Just refers to when he notes that: 'the Revolution is frozen'.

In other words, the category of failure is not relevant here, for it invariably consists in assessing the political sequence in terms of states of affairs that are external and heterogeneous to it. There is no failure, there is termination: a political sequence begins and comes to an end without being able to gauge the genuine intellectual power that either precedes or follows on from it. From this point of view, Thermidor cannot be the name for the meaning of the Terror. It is the name for what is arrived at once what Sylvain Lazarus calls the revolutionary political mode has been terminated.

My objective will therefore be to appoint 'Thermidorean' as the name of a subjectivity that is both singular and typical; the subjectivity that deploys itself within the space of termination.

It is crucial to clarify the status of my approach, which has nothing to do with historiography. Although I will cite the Thermidoreans of 1794 as examples, I will not consider them as particular figures in a history of the State. There are some very fine books that do just that, of which Mathiez's *Réaction thermidorienne*[6] heads the field. But neither will my approach consist in considering politics as thought. Sylvain Lazarus tirelessly repeats that politics provides the basis for a thought of politics. But unlike the revolutionary sequence of 1792–94, it is difficult to consider the Thermidorean Convention as a singular political sequence. And even if it were possible, the latter would then have to be thought on its own terms, in which case 'Thermidorean' would be the name of a singularity, rather than a possible generic concept.

My approach here will be philosophical. It is a question of turning the adjective 'Thermidorean' into a concept: the concept of the subjectivity constituted through the termination of a political sequence. This concept will be incorporated into a philosophy that is conditioned by emancipatory instances of politics or, as Lazarus would put it, by those politics that operate 'in interiority'. Which also means: a philosophy conditioned by the rare and discontinuous character of such instances, by their inevitable termination, which nothing can *sublate*.

We are all familiar with Saint-Just's fundamental question: what do they want, those who want neither virtue nor terror? It is this enigmatic will that appropriates termination. Its object is a State, a State withdrawn from every prescription of virtue, and whose explicitly avowed terroristic dimension is entirely different from terror in its revolutionary Jacobin sense, the crucial difference being that the principle of virtue is replaced by the principle of interest.

The exemplary Thermidorean, the one who provides the definitive formulation of the generic figure of the Thermidorean, is without doubt Boissy d'Anglas. His great canonical text is the discourse of 5 Messidor Year III. Let us quote a key passage:

> We should be governed by the best ... [Y]et, with very few exceptions, you will find such men only among those who, owning property, are bound to the country in which it lies, to the laws that protect it, to the peace that preserves it ...[7]

Virtue is an unconditioned subjective prescription, one that refers to no other objective determination. This is why Boissy d'Anglas rejects it: he does not require leaders to be virtuous politicians, only that they be governmental representatives of the 'best'. But 'best' does not constitute a subjective determination. It is a well-defined category, one that is absolutely conditioned by the objective figure of property. Boissy d'Anglas puts forward three reasons for handing the State over to the 'best'. These reasons are crucial and have a great future before them:

- For a Thermidorean, a *country* is not a possible place for Republican virtues, as it is for the Jacobin patriot. It is what contains a property. A country is an economic objectivity.
- For a Thermidorean, the *law* is not a maxim derived from the relation between principles and the situation, as it is for the Jacobin. It is what provides protection, and specifically what protects property. In this regard, its universality is entirely secondary. What counts is *its function*.
- For a Thermidorean, *insurrection* cannot be the most sacred of duties, as it is for a Jacobin whenever the universality of principles is trampled over. The property owner's central and legitimate demand is for peace.

Here we find the triad of an objective conception of the country, a conservative conception of law, and a security-obsessed conception of situations. Thus, our initial description of the concept of the Thermidorean sees in the latter an alliance between objectivism, the 'natural' *status quo*, and the preoccupation with security.

We know that, for Saint-Just, the opposite of virtue is corruption. And a consideration of the nature of corruption seems apposite today. Sylvain Lazarus has shown that 'corruption' initially designates the precariousness of politics. This precariousness is a consequence of the fact that the real principle of politics is subjective (virtue or principles). It is only after the fact, and by way of consequences, that we uncover material corruption. A Thermidorean is essentially politically corrupt – in other words, he exploits the precariousness of political convictions. But then, in politics, there are only convictions (and wills).

It is clearly the case, moreover, that the Thermidoreans of 1794 are also corrupt in the contemporary sense, and it is no coincidence that they assume political centre-stage following the exit of the Incorruptible: there is the financial backing from the English, which they drew upon in abundance; the shameless profiteering from national resources; the monopolising of grain; the military pillaging (for Thermidor also marks the passage from a principled and defensive Republican war to a war of rapine and conquest) and the trafficking in army supplies. But above all, there are the close ties with the colonialists and slave traders, on which fresh light is thrown by Florence Gauthier's book *Triomphe et mort du droit naturel en révolution*.[8] In it we re-encounter Boissy d'Anglas who, on 17 Thermidor Year III, gives a major speech in which he argues against any notion of independence for the colonies. His argument will prove influential for almost two centuries and is still employed today by Pascal Bruckner when the latter, in his very Thermidorean *The Tears of the White Man*,[9] sets out publicly to wash his hands of everything that happens to the people and countries of 'the third world': colonised peoples are not 'mature' enough for independence (i.e. they are responsible for their own rather unfortunate and undemocratic poverty). The only thing these people may aspire to is a closely monitored domestic autonomy (i.e. a development controlled by the IMF, provided they are able to demonstrate genuine progress in the 'modern democratic' spirit). Here is Boissy d'Anglas again:

Far from aspiring to a freedom the conquest and preservation of which would cost them too much effort, they luxuriate complacently in the opulence and pleasures that freedom brings ... [N]either sword nor ploughshare will ever roughen their hands. Such a people must therefore remain content with being subject to wise and peaceful government by just and humane men who are enemies of tyranny.[10]

For Boissy d'Anglas, there can never be too many institutional checks to control these peoples who remain largely incapable of any 'effort' towards freedom. Yet it is curious to note that these institutional controls invoke the power of law to 'pacify' the 'revolutionary movement' in these supposedly sleepy colonies:

We propose that these colonies be divided into different departments, and that, as in your own local departments, an administration comprising five members and invested with the same functions and subject to the same laws be put in place there. But since this part of France is still caught up in a revolutionary movement which only the habit of freedom and the power of your laws can pacify, it is our conviction that you should issue a provisional decree stipulating until such a time as your successors prescribe otherwise that these administrators be appointed by the Executive Directory.[11]

In fact, Boissy d'Anglas' sole concern is to satisfy his planter and slave trader friends, in accordance with the three maxims espoused by the exemplary Thermidorean: the colonies belong to France because we have property there; the law must 'pacify' the independence movement's emancipatory fervour because it threatens this property; and finally, direct administrative control of these colonies is desirable because our security is at stake.

But once again, this material and legislative corruption is merely secondary. Even today, in both France and Italy, we see

how the attempt to deal with corruption at an exclusively empirical and legal level threatens to replace petty crooks and pushers
with far more powerful criminals and hardened black-marketeers.
The idea that you can replace dirty money with clean with the
help of a few judges is risible. It is entirely legitimate to stipu-
late axiomatically that, beyond a certain sum, when one starts
calculating in tens of millions, all capitalist money is bound to
be dirty. If it were possible to handle such quantities of the
general equivalent ingenuously, we would know it by now. No,
the theme of corruption only becomes real when one grasps it
fundamentally as the irrecusable weakness of politics. What lies
at the heart of the Thermidorean question is not the rather
obvious way in which Thermidorean politicians depended on
the colonial lobby, financial speculators and pillaging generals.
The heart of the matter is attained once we recognise that for
every Thermidorean, whether from 1794 or the present day, the
category of virtue is declared to be *devoid of political force*. Virtue
is an unsustainable effort that necessarily leads to the worst:
Terror. Here is Boissy d'Anglas once more: 'The man without
property ... must ceaselessly strive toward virtue so as to sustain
an interest in the order that safeguards him nothing...'.[12]

First, note here how political subjectivity is referred back to
order, rather than to the possibility of bringing about that which
is latent in a situation, under some maxim or other. This counter-
revolutionary swing could be called the *statification* of political
consciousness. To grasp its exact opposite, it should be enough
to recall the principle of Mao Tse-tung: 'Unrest is an excellent
thing.'

Second, note how for Boissy d'Anglas 'to take an interest in'
implies (objective) interest. In this case, the name of the interest
is 'property'. But, at a more formal level, there is the idea that
an interest lies at the heart of *every* subjective demand. Today,

this continues to be the principal and perhaps the only argument used in favour of the market economy.

Against 'the constant striving toward virtue', which is the very principle of all politics as far as the great Jacobins are concerned, Boissy d'Anglas endorses the connection between State (order) and interest. There is a shift away from striving, towards interestedness.

Thus, my contention is that Thermidorean subjectivity, which is grounded in the termination of a politics, carries out this coupling between State and interest. It is this coupling which certifies that political prescription (which in this instance is called 'virtue') is absent from now on.

In my philosophical vocabulary, this arrangement can be summarised as follows:

- The centre of gravity is no longer the situation, but the state of the situation.
- The subjective path is no longer governed by a maxim, and by the statements that become related to it according to the test of situations. It is governed by the interest one has in the statified order. Which is also to say: what counts is no longer the aleatory trajectory of a truth, but the calculable trajectory of an inclusion. Whereas every trajectory of truth is a singular work dependent upon an event's supernumerary dimension, the trajectory of interest remains coextensive with situational placement. As a subject, the Thermidorean is constitutively *in search of a place*.

This being the case, the term 'Thermidorean' is not a structural designation referring to the secondary branch of an alternative wherein 'truth procedure', or 'generic procedure', features as the primary branch. 'Thermidorean' designates the triad of statification, calculable interest and placement whose termination is *conditioned by* a non-dialectisable truth procedure.

The fact that the revolutionary political mode took place between 1792 and 1794 and terminated on 9 Thermidor is constitutive of Thermidorean subjectivity as singularity. Statification, calculable interest and placement are merely the formal features of this singularity. And in order to think this singularity we have to think termination.

Let me now try to clarify my elaboration of the concept of the Thermidorean by showing how the subjectivity referred to (from 1976 onwards) with the name 'new philosophers', or 'new philosophy', merits such a designation.

There can be no doubt that what is known as 'the new philosophy' exhibits the following formal features:

- Statification took the form of rallying behind the parliamentary process, and of indifference to non-statist situations; at best it took the form of peaceful coexistence and, at worst, active complicity with Mitterrandism.
- Calculable interest took the form of self-abasement on the part of intellectuals, who abandoned every inventive political prescription, every genuinely progressive, critical function, in an attempt to make inroads into the realms of the mass media and the institution.
- Placement took the form of a wholly conservative mode of argument, which, under the banner of 'human rights', contrasts the excellence of Western democracy with the abominable totalitarianism of the East.

This is no more than an analogy, since it is questionable to what extent the intense period of direct political activism between 1965 and 1975 constituted a genuine political mode. But this analogy does at least allow us to demonstrate some of the characteristic ways in which these formal features *intertwine*. For the new philosophers did indeed arise from the well-documented termination of a sequence: the 'leftist', 'Maoist' or '68' sequence. This implies:

- That they themselves were the protagonists of the sequence in question. All the notorious new philosophers are former Maoists, and specifically former members of the Gauche Prolétarienne.[13] Similarly, the Thermidoreans of 1794 were not foreign aristocrats, restorers or even Girondins. They were part of the Robespierrist majority in the Convention.
- That the judgement about what the sequence was is constitutive of the way in which the formal Thermidorean features are invested. This judgement is based on a *disarticulation* of statements from the sequence. The militancy of the years 1965–75 brought about an organic link between a certain brand of activism and ideological principles at the heart of which lay the people ('serve the people'), the figure of the worker, and the Real of the factories. The Thermidorean renegades of the 1980s separated activism from every principle and every situation, and pretended that this activism was only ever connected with the Chinese or Soviet States. How else are we to explain the thoroughly irrational fact that the 'discovery' of Solzhenitsyn seems to be all the proof these Thermidorean new philosophers needed? What is the relation between the Stalinist camps of the 1930s and the blind and magnificent path that led thousands of young students to the factories of France? Or between Stalinism and the multiform invention of new practices of declaration, demonstration and organisation? This relation is simply the construction of a non-relation, a disarticulation. Once

severed from its real content, 'leftist' activism (which the
Thermidoreans of 1794 were also heartily sick of) is filed
alongside subjective pathology and fascination with totalitarian statism, a classification that does indeed render it
absolutely unintelligible. That unintelligibility is an effect of
disarticulation. But the unintelligibility of a terminated
sequence is quite singular.

Thus, the singularisation of the formal features is achieved by
way of a disarticulation of the political sequence. This disarticulation produces something unintelligible. And producing the
unthinkable is precisely what it's about, so that thought itself
becomes discredited and only the existing state of things remains.

We will say that 'Thermidorean' names the subjectivity which,
whenever a political sequence terminates, renders it distinctly
unthinkable through the disarticulation of its statements, and to
the profit of statification, calculable interest and placement.

The unintelligibility of the sequence invariably signifies the
concurrent eviction of thought, specifically from the political
field, *because the sequence is precisely what there is to think*. This is how,
as far as popular opinion is concerned, the category of totalitarianism, along with its accompanying emphasis on human
rights (which certain new philosophers took it upon themselves
to 'found') rendered the works of Lenin and Mao Tse-tung
unthinkable during a prolonged period, just as it occluded the
militant inventions of the 1960s and 1970s. As a result, the
sequences 1902–17, 1920–47 and 1965–75, which provide a
discontinuous summary of the history of twentieth-century
politics, became unintelligible singularities.

Boissy d'Anglas himself works assiduously to render the
revolutionary sequence unintelligible. In order to do this, he
reduces it to a 'violent convulsion' brought about as a result of

the popular masses' economic incompetence (an argument which still runs rife):

> If you grant unconditional political rights to men without property, then should the latter come to occupy the benches of the legislators, they will incite or let others incite unrest with no concern for the consequences; they will implement or permit the implementation of taxes that are injurious to commerce and agriculture because they will not have felt, or feared, or foreseen the dreadful consequences, and they will ultimately plunge us back into the violent convulsions from which we have only just escaped ... [14]

The framework which Boissy d'Anglas delineates here links the irrationality of the situation (violent convulsions) to the irrationality of the protagonists (those without property flout the 'laws of the economy'). He thereby renders the revolutionary sequence politically unthinkable. The disarticulation consists in using a principle of interest to separate terror (here referred to as 'violence') from virtue. Similarly, the new philosophers used a statist principle of illusion to separate leftist activism from its real content (thereby proceeding, against all available evidence, as though the subjective 'motor' of activism had been a set of illusory beliefs about the socialist States).

That this framework exerts a tenacious hold on thought is confirmed, not just by its continual redeployment in periods of conservative reaction, but also by the way it has made its presence felt within Marxist historiography as such. For the attempts to make the economy the heart of the problem, to do away with political singularities, and to transform the avatars of taxation into the alpha and omega of critical analysis were all increasingly important factors in the academic Marxist analysis of the Revolution which animated the French Communist Party during the 1950s, but which today sound like nothing so much as the return of Boissy d'Anglas. Consider by way of evidence this staggering remark of Soboul's: 'The 9 Thermidor doesn't mark a break [*coupure*], but an acceleration.'

When all is said and done, 'Thermidorean' is the name for that which, whenever a truth procedure terminates, renders that procedure unthinkable. We have just seen how this constitution of the unthinkable can have a long-lasting power. It provides the historical matrix for a destitution of thought.

Bearing this in mind, let us return to the Terror. In reality, when considered in isolation, 'terror' functions as one of the disarticulated terms of the unthinkable. The attempt to 'think terror' is impractical as such, because the isolation of the category of terror is precisely a Thermidorean operation (as is the attempt to think the socialist States solely on the basis of their terroristic dimension). It is an operation designed to produce something unintelligible and unthinkable. Considered in isolation, terror becomes an infra-political datum, one that is politically unthinkable, thereby leaving the terrain wide open for moralistic preaching against acts of violence. By the same token, because it renders politics unthinkable, the disarticulation of the leftist sequence is the true source of humanitarian preaching, of ethics, and of the liberal-democratic premium on 'human rights'.

What is subtracted from the Thermidorean operation is something other than a clumsy attempt at justifying or elucidating the nature of terror considered 'in itself'. To proceed in this way would be to accept the unthinkable realm inhabited by the Thermidorean. We must examine the revolutionary work as a homogeneous multiplicity wherein terror functions as an *inseparable* category, and specifically as one that is inseparable from virtue.

In politics, and where the French Revolution is concerned, the precondition for all thought consists in undoing the

Thermidorean framework, which, it has to be said, is also very often the Marxist framework. Soboul paved the way for Furet.

And in philosophy? We would have to investigate the following difficult question: when a truth procedure terminates, is it *invariably* affected by the production of that which is unthinkable? Is thought obliged to endure Thermidorean frameworks of its own ruination?

Best to leave this question unanswered for the time being. By way of conclusion, let us delineate something positive instead: the ontological characteristics of the political procedure.

Notes

1 A version of this text was originally published as 'Qu'est-ce qu'un thermidorien?', in Catherine Kintzler and Hadi Risk eds., *La République et la terreur*, Paris: Kimé, 1996, pp. 53–64.

2 Badiou is talking about Stéphane Courtois et al., *The Black Book of Communism: Crimes, Terror, Repression*, trans. Jonathan Murphy and ed. Mark Kramer. Cambridge, Mass.: Harvard University Press, 1999. *Trans.*

3 G. (L.G.) Duval, *Souvenirs thermidoriens*, 2 vols. Paris: Victor Magen, 1844.

4 *Constitution de la République Française proposée au peuple français par la Convention Nationale*, Paris: Fructidor, an III.

5 Albert Soboul, 1914–82. French communist historian and holder of the chair of the History of the Revolution at the Sorbonne. *Trans.*

6 Albert Mathiez, *La Réaction Thermidorienne*, Paris: Librairie Armand Colin, 1929.

7 *Projet de Constitution pour la République Française et Discours Préliminaire prononcé par Boissy d'Anglas au nom de la Commission des Onze, dans la*

séance du 5 messidor, an 3, Paris: Imprimé par ordre de la Convention Nationale, an III, pp. 27–8.

8 Florence Gauthier, *Triomphe et mort du droit naturel en Révolution 1789–1795–1802*, Paris: Presses Universitaires de France, 1992.

9 Pascal Bruckner, *The Tears of the White Man*, trans. William R. Beer. London: Collier Macmillan, 1986. [*Le Sanglot de l'homme blanc. Tiers Monde, culpabilité, haine de soi*, Paris: Seuil, 1983.]

10 *Rapport et projet d'articles constitutionnels relatifs aux Colonies Présentés à la Convention Nationale, au nom de la Commission des Onze, par Boissy d'Anglas, dans la séance du 17 Thermidor, an III*, Paris: Imprimé par ordre de la Convention Nationale, an III, p. 4.

11 Ibid., p. 9.

12 *Projet de Constitution pour la République Française*, p. 28.

13 The Gauche Prolétarienne (GP), or 'Proletarian Left', was an ultra-leftist organisation, set up in 1968 in the immediate aftermath of the May events, among whose ranks were counted André Glucksmann and Michel Le Bris, and whose official newspaper, *La Cause du Peuple*, was edited by Jean-Paul Sartre. *Trans.*

14 *Projet de Constitution pour la République Française*, p. 28.

Politics as Truth Procedure

When, and under what conditions, can an event be said to be political? What is the 'what happens' insofar as it happens politically?

We will maintain that an event is political, and that the procedure it engages exhibits a political truth, only under certain conditions. These conditions pertain to the material of the event, to the infinite, to its relation to the state of the situation, and to the numericality of the procedure.

1. An event is political if its material is collective, or if the event can only be attributed to a collective multiplicity. 'Collective' is not a numerical concept here. We say that the event is ontologically collective to the extent that it provides the vehicle for a virtual summoning of all. 'Collective' means immediately universalising. The effectiveness of politics relates to the affirmation according to which 'for every x, there is thought'.

By 'thought', I mean any truth procedure *considered subjectively*. 'Thought' is the name for the subject of a truth procedure. The use of the term 'collective' is an acknowledgement that if this thought is political, it belongs to all. It is not simply a question of address, as it is in the case of other types of truth. Of course, every truth is addressed to all. But in the case of politics, the universality is intrinsic, and not simply a function of the address. In politics, the possibility of the thought that identifies a subject is at every moment available to all. Those that are constituted as subject of a politics are called the *militants* of the procedure. But 'militant' is a category without borders, a subjective determination without identity, or without concept. That the political event is collective prescribes that all are the virtual militants of the thought that proceeds on the basis of the event. In this sense, politics is the sole truth procedure that is not only generic in its result, but also in the local composition of its subject.

Only politics is intrinsically required to declare that the thought that it is is the thought of all. This declaration is its constitutive prerequisite. All that the mathematician requires, for instance, is at least one other mathematician to recognise the validity of his proof. In order to assure itself of the thought that it is, love need only assume the two. The artist ultimately needs no one. Science, art and love are aristocratic truth procedures. Of course, they are addressed to all and universalise their own singularity. But their regime is not that of the collective. Politics is impossible without the statement that people, taken indistinctly, are capable of the thought that constitutes the post-evental political subject. This statement claims that a political thought is topologically collective, meaning that it cannot exist otherwise than as the thought of all.

That the central activity of politics is the *meeting* is a local metonymy of its intrinsically collective, and therefore principally universal, being.

2. The effect of the collective character of the political event is that politics presents as such the infinite character of situations. Politics summons or exhibits the infinity of the situation. Every politics of emancipation rejects finitude, rejects 'being towards

death'. Since a politics includes in the situation the thought of all, it is engaged in rendering explicit the subjective infinity of situations.

Of course, every situation is ontologically infinite. But only politics summons this infinity immediately, as subjective universality.

Science, for example, is the capture of the void and the infinite by the letter. It has no concern for the subjective infinity of situations. Art presents the sensible in the finitude of a work, and the infinite only intervenes in it to the extent that the artist destines the infinite to the finite. But politics treats the infinite as such according to the principle of the same, the egalitarian principle. This is its point of departure: the situation is open, never closed, and the possible affects its immanent subjective infinity. We will say that the numericality of the political procedure has the infinite as its first term; whereas for love this first term is one; for science the void; and for art a finite number. The infinite comes into play in every truth procedure, but only in politics does it take first place. This is because only in politics is deliberation about the possible (and hence about the infinity of the situation) constitutive of the process itself.

3. Lastly, what is the relation between politics and the state of the situation, and more particularly between politics and the State, in both the ontological and historical senses of the term?

The state of the situation is the operation which, within the situation, codifies its parts or subsets. The state is a sort of meta-structure that exercises the power of counting over all the subsets of the situation. Every situation has a state. Every situation is the presentation of itself, of what composes it, of what belongs to it. But it is also given as state of the situation, that is, as the internal configuration of its parts or subsets, and therefore as re-presentation. More specifically, the state of the situation re-presents collective situations, whilst in the collective situations themselves, singularities are not re-presented but presented. On this point, I refer the reader to my *Being and Event*, Meditation 8.[1]

A fundamental datum of ontology is that the state of the situation always exceeds the situation itself. There are always more parts than elements, i.e. the representative multiplicity is always of a higher power than the presentative multiplicity. This question is really that of power. The power of the State is always superior to that of the situation. The State, and hence also the economy, which is today the norm of the State, are characterised by a structural effect of separation and superpower with regard to what is simply presented in the situation.

It has been mathematically demonstrated that this excess is not measurable. There is no answer to the question about *how much* the power of the State exceeds the individual, or how much the power of representation exceeds that of simple presentation. The excess is errant. The simplest experience of the relation to the State shows that one relates to it without ever being able to assign a measure to its power. The representation of the State by power, say public power, points on the one hand to its excess, and on the other to the indeterminacy or errancy of this excess.

We know that when politics exists, it immediately gives rise to a show of power by the State. This is obviously due to the fact that politics is collective, and hence universally concerns the parts of the situation, thereby encroaching upon the domain from which the state of the situation draws its existence. Politics summons the power of the State. Moreover, it is the only truth procedure to do so directly. The usual symptom of this summoning is the fact that politics invariably encounters repression. But repression, which is the empirical form of the errant superpower of the State, is not the essential point.

The real characteristic of the political event and the truth procedure that it sets off is that a political event fixes the errancy and assigns a measure to the superpower of the State. It fixes the power of the State. Consequently, the political event interrupts the subjective errancy of the power of the State. It configures the state of the situation. It gives it a figure; it configures its power; it measures it.

Empirically, this means that whenever there is a genuinely political event, the State reveals itself. It reveals its excess of power, its repressive dimension. But it also reveals a measure for this usually invisible excess. For it is essential to the normal functioning of the State that its power remains measureless, errant, unassignable. The political event puts an end to all this by assigning a visible measure to the excessive power of the State.

Politics puts the State at a distance, in the distance of its measure. The resignation that characterises a time without politics feeds on the fact that the State is not at a distance, because the measure of its power is errant. People are held hostage by its unassignable errancy. Politics is the interruption of this errancy. It exhibits a measure for statist power. This is the sense in which politics is 'freedom'. The State is in fact the measureless enslavement of the parts of the situation, an enslavement whose secret is precisely the errancy of superpower, its absence of measure. Freedom here consists in putting the State at a distance through the collective establishment of a measure for its excess. And if the excess if measured, it is because the collective can measure up to it.

We will call *political prescription* the post-evental establishment of a fixed measure for the power of the State.

We can now proceed to elaborate the numericality of the political procedure.

Why does every truth procedure possess a numericality? Because there is a determination of each truth's relation to the different types of multiple that singularise it: the situation, the state of the situation, the event and the subjective operation. This relation is expressed by a number (including Cantorian or infinite numbers). Thus, the procedure has an abstract schema, fixed in some typical numbers which encode the 'traversal' of the multiples that are ontologically constitutive of this procedure.

Let us give Lacan his due: he was the first to make a systematic use of numericality, whether it be a question of assigning the subject to zero as the gap between 1 and 2 (the subject is what falls between the primordial signifiers S1 and S2), or of the synthetic bearing of 3 (the Borromean knotting of the Real, the Symbolic and the Imaginary), or of the function of the infinite in feminine *jouissance*.

In the case of politics, we said that its first term, which is linked to the collective character of the political event, is the infinite of the situation. It is the simple infinite, the infinite of presentation. This infinite is determined; the value of its power is fixed.

We also said that politics necessarily summons the state of the situation, and therefore a second infinite. This second infinite is in excess of the first, its power is superior, but in general we cannot know by how much. The excess is measureless. We can therefore say that the second term of political numericality is a second infinite, the one of State power, and that all we can know about this infinite is that it is superior to the first, and that this difference remains undetermined. If we call σ the fixed infinite cardinality of the situation, and ε the cardinality that measures the power of the State, then apart from politics, we have no means of knowing anything other than: ε is superior to σ. This indeterminate superiority masks the alienating and repressive nature of the state of the situation.

The political event prescribes a measure to the measureless-ness of the State through the suddenly emergent materiality of a universalisable collective. It substitutes a fixed measure for the errant ε; one that almost invariably remains superior to the power σ of simple presentation, of course, but which is no longer endowed with the alienating and repressive powers of indeterminacy. We will use the expression $\pi(\varepsilon)$ to symbolise the result of the political prescription directed at the State.

The mark π designates the political function. It is exercised in several spaces (though we shall not go into the details here) correlated with the places of a singular politics ('places' in the sense defined by Sylvain Lazarus). This function is the trace left in the situation by the bygone political event. What concerns us here is its principal efficacy, which consists in interrupting the indeterminacy of statist power.

The first three terms of the numericality of the political procedure, all of which are infinite, are ultimately the following:

1. The infinity of the situation, which is summoned as such through the collective dimension of the political event, which is to say, through the supposition of the 'for all' of thought. We will refer to it as σ.

2. The infinity of the state of the situation, which is summoned by repression and alienation, because it supposedly controls all the collectives or subsets of the situation. It is an infinite cardinal number that remains indeterminate, though it is always superior to the infinite power of the situation whose state it is. We will therefore write: $\varepsilon > \sigma$.

3. The fixing by political prescription, under an evental and collective condition, of a measure for statist power. Through this prescription, the errancy of statist excess is interrupted and it becomes possible to use militant watchwords to practise and

calculate the free distance of political thinking from the State. We write this as $\pi(\epsilon)$, designating a determinate infinite cardinal number.

Let us try to clarify the fundamental operation of prescription by giving some examples. The Bolshevik insurrection of 1917 reveals a weak State, undermined by war, whereas tsarism was a paradigmatic instance of the quasi-sacred indeterminacy of the State's superpower. Generally speaking, insurrectionary forms of political thought are bound to a post-eventual determination of the power of the State as being very weak or even inferior to the power of simple collective presentation.

By way of contrast, the Maoist choice of protracted war and of the encirclement of the towns by the countryside prescribes to the State what is still an elevated measure of its power and carefully calculates the free distance from this power. This is the real reason why Mao's question remains the following: why can China's red political power exist? Or, how can the weakest prevail over the strongest in the long run? Which is to say that, for Mao, $\pi(\epsilon)$ – understood as the prescription concerning the power of the State – remains largely superior to the σ infinity of the situation such that it is summoned by the political procedure.

This is to say that the first three components of numericality – the three infinites σ, ϵ, $\pi(\epsilon)$ – are affected by each singular political sequence and do not have any sort of fixed determination, save for that of their mutual relations. More specifically, every politics proceeds to its own post-eventual prescription vis-à-vis the power of the State, so that it essentially consists in creating the political function π in the wake of the eventual upsurge.

When the political procedure exists, such that it manages a prescription vis-à-vis the State, then and only then can the logic of the same, or the egalitarian maxim proper to every politics of emancipation, be set out.

For the egalitarian maxim is effectively incompatible with the errancy of statist excess. The matrix of inequality consists precisely in the impossibility of measuring the superpower of the State. Today, for example, it is in the name of a necessity of the liberal economy – a necessity without measure or concept – that every egalitarian politics is deemed to be impossible and declared absurd. But what characterises this blind power of unfettered Capital is precisely the fact that it cannot be either measured or fixed at any point. All we know is that it prevails absolutely over the subjective fate of collectives, regardless of who they are. Thus, in order for a politics to be able to practise an egalitarian maxim in the sequence opened by an event, it is absolutely necessary that the state of the situation be put at a distance through a strict determination of its power.

Non-egalitarian consciousness is a mute consciousness, the captive of an errancy, of a power which it cannot measure. This is what explains the arrogant and peremptory character of non-egalitarian statements, even when they are obviously inconsistent and abject. For the statements of contemporary reaction are shored up entirely by the errancy of statist excess, i.e. by the untrammelled violence of capitalist anarchy. This is why liberal statements combine certainty about power with total indecision about its consequences for people's lives and the universal affirmation of collectives.

Egalitarian logic can only begin when the State is configured, put at a distance, measured. It is the errancy of the excess that impedes egalitarian logic, not the excess itself. It is not the simple power of the state of the situation that prohibits egalitarian politics. It is the obscurity and measurelessness in which this power is enveloped. If the political event allows for a clarification, a fixation, an exhibition of this power, then the egalitarian maxim is at least locally practicable.

But what is the figure for this equality, the figure for the prescription whereby each and every singularity is to be treated collectively and identically in political thought? This figure is obviously the 1. Finally to count as one that which is not even counted is what is at stake in every genuinely political thought, every prescription that summons the collective as such. The 1 is the numericality of the same, and to produce the same is what an emancipatory political procedure is capable of. The 1 disfigures every non-egalitarian claim.

To produce the same, to count each one universally as one, it is necessary to work *locally*, in the gap opened up between politics and the State, a gap whose principle resides in the measure $\pi(\varepsilon)$. This is how a Maoist politics was able to experiment with an agrarian revolution in the liberated zones (those beyond the reach of the reactionary armies), or a Bolshevik politics was able to effect a partial transfer of certain statist operations into the hands of the Soviets, at least in those instances where the latter were capable of assuming them. What is at work in such situations is once again the political function π, applied under the conditions of the prescriptive distance it has itself created, but this time with the aim of producing the same, or producing the Real in accordance with an egalitarian maxim. One will therefore write: $\pi(\pi(\varepsilon)) \Rightarrow 1$ in order to designate this doubling of the political function which works to produce equality under the conditions of freedom of thought/practice opened up by the fixation of statist power.

We can now complete the numericality of the political procedure. It is composed of three infinites: that of the situation; that of the state of the situation, which is indeterminate; and that of the prescription, which interrupts the indeterminacy and allows for a distance to be taken vis-à-vis the State. This numericality is completed by the 1, which is partially engendered by the political function under the conditions of the distance from the State, which themselves derive from this function. Here, the 1 is the figure of equality and sameness.

The numericality is written as follows: $\sigma, \varepsilon, \pi(\varepsilon), \pi(\pi(\varepsilon)) \Rightarrow 1$.

What singularises the political procedure is the fact that it proceeds from the infinite to the 1. It makes the 1 of equality arise as the universal truth of the collective by carrying out a prescriptive operation upon the infinity of the State; an operation whereby it constructs its own autonomy, or distance, and is able to effectuate its maxim from within that distance.

Conversely, let us note in passing that, as I established in *Conditions*,[2] the amorous procedure, which deploys the truth of difference or sexuation (rather than of the collective), proceeds from the 1 to the infinite through the mediation of the two. In this sense – and I leave the reader to meditate upon this – politics is love's numerical inverse. In other words: love begins where politics ends.

And since the term 'democracy' is today decisive, let me conclude by providing my own definition of it, one in which its identity with politics will be rendered legible.

Democracy consists in the always singular adjustment of freedom and equality. But what is the moment of freedom in politics? It is the one wherein the State is put at a distance, and hence the one wherein the political function π operates as the assignation of a measure to the errant superpower of the state of the situation. And what is equality, if not the operation whereby, in the distance thus created, the political function is applied once again, this time so as to produce the 1? Thus, for a determinate political procedure, the political adjustment of freedom and equality is nothing but the adjustment of the last two terms of its numericality.

It is written: $[\pi(\varepsilon)\!-\!\pi(\pi(\varepsilon)) \Rightarrow 1]$.

It should go without saying that what we have here is the notation of democracy. Our two examples show that this notation has had singular names: 'Soviets' during the Bolshevik revolution, 'liberated zones' during the Maoist process. But democracy has had many other names in the past. It has some in the present (for example: 'gathering of the Organisation Politique and of the collective of illegal immigrant workers from the hostels'); and it will have others in the future.

Despite its rarity, politics – and hence democracy – has existed, exists and will exist. And alongside it, under its demanding condition, metapolitics – which is what a philosophy declares, with its own effects in mind, to be worthy of the name 'politics'. Or alternatively, what a thought declares to be a thought, and under whose condition it thinks what a thought is.

Notes

1 Alain Badiou, *L'Être et l'événement*, Paris: Seuil, 1988, pp. 109–19.

2 Alain Badiou, 'Qu'est-ce que l'amour', in *Conditions*, Paris: Seuil, 1992; translated as 'What is Love?' by Justin Clemens in *Umbr(a): A Journal of the Unconscious* 1, 1996; reprinted in R. Salecl ed., *Sexuation*. Durham, NC: Duke University Press, 2000, pp. 263–81.

Index

A NOTE ON THE TYPE

The original punches of the types cut by John Baskervillle of Birmingham were sold by Baskerville's widow to Beaumarchais and descended through various French foundaries to Beberny and Peignot. Some of the material survives and is now at the Cambridge University Press. Baskerville has been called the first of the transitional romans in England. Compared with Caslon there is more differentiation of thick and thin strokes, the serifs on the lower-case letters are more nearly horizontal and the stress nearer the vertical.

Ethics

An Essay on the Understanding of Evil
ALAIN BADIOU

Translated by Peter Hallward

Paperback | 85984 435 9
$16/£12/$24CAN
224 pages • 5.5 × 7.5 inches

'Scarcely any other moral thinker of our day is as politically clear-sighted and courageously polemical, so prepared to put notions of truth and universality back on our agenda ... Badiou has launched a transformative new intervention, which deserves to provoke a persisting response.' *Terry Eagleton*

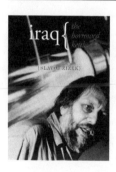

Iraq
The Borrowed Kettle
SLAVOJ ŽIŽEK

Paperback | 84467 540 8
$16/£8.99/$23CAN
192 pages • 5.5 × 7.5 inches

'Žižek leaves no social or natural phenomenon untheorized, and is master of the counter-intuitive observation.' *New Yorker*

'Žižek has the knack of conjuring the most audacious conclusions between politics, popular culture and high theory.' *Time Out*

NEW FROM VERSO

Archaeologies of the Future
The Desire Called Utopia and Other Science Fictions
FREDRIC JAMESON

September 2005

Hardback 1 84467 033 3
$35/£20/$49CAN
480 pages • 6 × 9 inches

'There is no better example of a "Marxist scholastic" than Fredric Jameson.'
The Economist

Books for Burning
Between Civil War and Democracy in 1970s Italy
ANTONIO NEGRI

Edited by Timothy S Murphy
Translated by Arianna Bove, Ed Emery,
Timothy S Murphy and Francesco Novello

September 2005

Paperback Original 1 84467 034 1
$25/£16/$35CAN
336 pages • 6 × 9 inches

PRAISE FOR *MULTITUDE*
'Far left thinking with clarity, measured reasoning and humour, major accomplishments
in and of themselves.' *Publishers Weekly*

NEW FROM VERSO

Afflicted Powers
Capital and Spectacle in a New Age of War
RETORT

June 2005

Paperback Original | 84467 031 7
$16/£9.99/$24CAN
224 pages • 5.5 × 7.5 inches

'A comprehensive analysis of America's relationship with the world. No stone is left unturned. The maggots exposed are grotesque.' *Harold Pinter*

Critique of Everyday Life
Volume III: From Modernity to Modernism
HENRI LEFEBVRE

Translated by Gregory Elliott
Preface by Michael Trebitsch

January 2006

Hardback | 85984 590 8
$30/£16.99/$42CAN
208 pages • 6 × 9 inches

'A savage critique of consumerist society.' *Publishers Weekly*

'A brilliant example of how theory can be joined with experience to critique and better understand contemporary society.' *Frontlist*

MORE TITLES AVAILABLE FROM VERSO